HOTEL SUCCESS HANDBOOK

www.HotelSuccessHandbook.com

HOTEL SUCCESS HANDBOOK

Practical sales and marketing actions, ideas and tips to get results for your small hotel, B&B, or guest accommodation

Caroline Cooper
&
Lucy Whittington

www.HotelSuccessHandbook.com

First edition published in 2010

Paperback ISBN 9781904312888
Published in the UK by MX Publishing
335 Princess Park Manor, Royal Drive, London, N11 3GX

Dedications

Caroline dedicates this book to Clive, her husband, for putting up with too many late dinners, and her Dad for all his encouragement.

Lucy dedicates this book to her family – husband Andy for his ongoing support, encouragement & hot chocolates, and her small people Alex & Henry for their smiles.

Praise

"I wish I'd had this book to hand when I started out."
"If you do not want to be the laughing stock of the next series of The Hotel Inspector *you will want to read this book – from start to finish."*

Thomas Dowson, B&B owner
www.bassecopette.com

"Devoid of sales and marketing jargon, this handbook is just what every manager needs ready to hand and to be dipped into regularly. The Hotel Success Handbook is an essential addition to the hospitality manager's tool kit. "

Philippe Rossiter MBA FIH FTS, Chief Executive, Institute of Hospitality

"Although I hate to admit it I learnt an awful lot and found it an addictive page turner."

Patrick Burfield, Award Winning Restaurateur and Hotelier

"It really is a 'bible' for the twenty-tens and I defy anyone to come up with something that is not between the covers that should be included. Running a small business in tourism and hospitality just got a bit less scary."

David Curtis-Brignell, Chairman, The Tourism Society (2004-7)

"I can't recommend this book highly enough for any hotel owner looking to maximise not just the results they get from their web marketing, but their overall business growth and development."

Ed Rivis, author of Email Marketing Dynamite and The Ultimate Web Marketing Strategy

"This is a great book to have around - like having a brainstorming team and personal business advisor constantly on hand."
"A thorough and comprehensive guide"

Joy Huter 5* Bed and Breakfast owner

"An indispensable tool for small hotel and accommodation business owners who want an accessible guide to both traditional and online marketing."

Dr Philip Alford, Senior Lecturer Tourism & Hospitality Marketing, Bournemouth University

"This handbook provides all the relevant information for selling and marketing small hospitality businesses in an easy-to-read and easy-to-find format. "

Bob Cotton OBE, Chief Executive, British Hospitality Association

Acknowledgements

Our thanks go to the following people who have helped us so much with their support, encouragement and direction in putting this book together:

Andy Wilkes for all his input on anything design or web related (not to mention designing and building our website www.HotelSuccessHandbook.com)

Steve Emecz at MX publishing for his patience, publicity and advice www.mxpublishing.co.uk

Bob Gibson at Staunch Design for the book cover www.staunch.com

Ali Turnbull for her brilliant copy-editing, which made our words make sense www.fit-to-print.co.uk

Sally Shalam for her wonderfully written Foreword www.sallyshalam.com

Helen Stothard for last minute proof reading www.hlsbs.co.uk

Everyone who took the time to read through the book and provide us with such positive testimonials and encouraging feedback

And finally many thanks also to all our business friends and colleagues who offered their support, ideas, feedback and reality checks - online, offline and face to face. We're very grateful!

Contents

Foreword

By Sally Shalam, Hotel Critic, The Guardian

Every so often in the course of reviewing small, independent hotels and bed and breakfasts in Britain, I find I have discovered a newcomer which is a complete stunner, whose owners have ensured all the boxes are ticked. The sort of place which makes me want to punch the air with sheer delight, phone my Mum, then tell all my friends to come *right away*. Alas, as any experienced hotelier will tell you, fulfilling and exceeding guest expectation is only part of the path to long-lasting success.

For the would-be hotelier, and for the down-shifter dreaming about leaving the rat race, and setting up a B&B in the country, there is a lot to learn. Being a people person is, of course, essential, and possession of this quality is probably what attracts many to this industry in the first place. Hospitality, however, requires far more than that. It is an art. It is the art of dealing with whatever the day throws at you with charm and aplomb. It is about exceeding your guests' expectations and building a fine reputation. If that were not enough, you must also understand, in a competitive world, how to price yourself right and market your business successfully to the right people, keeping up with and embracing new technology.

A mediocre outfit which has a firm grip on marketing techniques and social media is probably more likely to see a sustained healthy return than an utterly sublime hotel of which no one has ever heard. In a world where branding is crucially important, owners of small hotels, B&Bs, all manner of guest accommodation, who fail to market themselves, are leaving a lot to chance. So while you're planning how to bring your stamp, your style, your vision into the exciting arena of the modern British hotel, this book will serve as the reality check, a handbook to guide you through the marketing maze while you're realising your dream.

www.sallyshalam.com

Sally Shalam writes a weekly review in Guardian Travel, specialising in small, independently owned accommodation in Britain, has her own UK page in Condé Nast Traveller and is a judge for Enjoy England's Awards for Excellence.

Preface

Although we have used the term 'hotel' throughout, we've written this book for owners and managers of any small independent hotel, bed and breakfast, restaurant with rooms, guesthouse or inn. Whether you run a seaside holiday hotel, business event accommodation, an idyllic wedding venue, or simply a convenient place for an overnight stay, this book can help you. Each chapter gives practical advice and a step-by-step guide to achieving increased occupancy and sales to help you achieve greater success for your hotel.

The *Hotel Success Handbook* is based on the business, marketing, training and operations knowledge and experience of Caroline Cooper and Lucy Whittington.

Caroline's training and business advice for hotels and restaurants comes from more than 25 years experience in the hospitality industry. Having run her own coaching and training company for the past five years means she also understands the day-to-day challenges of a small business.

Caroline is a qualified business coach, holds Member status of the Institute of Hospitality (MIH), and is a committee member of the BHA (British Hospitality Association).

Lucy's marketing career spans start-ups to plcs, and she now runs her own website design and marketing business. Combining a passion for travel with her love of marketing (especially online) her actions and tips for hotels are both researched and practical.

Lucy holds Member status of the Chartered Institute of Marketing (MCIM), has an MBA and is a consultant Member of the Tourism Society (MTS).

Lucy and Caroline work together to combine their experience and knowledge of marketing and sales, so that you – as a hotel owner or manager – get no-nonsense and practical advice, which you can use right away.

So let's get started!

Introduction

We've all seen the signs:

2 for 1

Rooms from £39.50

50% discount

You might even have made these offers yourself.

But slashing your room rates or offering half-price meals is not the best way to increased profits.

Don't just compete on price

Price might initially seem like an obvious way to attract more sales. It's easy to be the 'cheapest' or even the 'most expensive' but this is a hard game to play. You might easily sacrifice profit for your difference *(too cheap)* or you might be turning away guests *(too expensive or not offering perceived value for money).*

So whether we are talking meals, function packages or hotel rooms, slashing your rates to get increased sales or occupancy is **not** the best way to generate higher sales margins. As a short term measure it can help cash flow, and increase sales, but longer term it will have a negative impact on your guests' perception of quality and a massive impact on your margins. And once you have cut your prices, what happens when you want to put them up again?

We're not saying never give discounts, but we suggest that if you do ever discount leave scope to upsell on other products or services.

The good news is there are plenty of other strategies you can use to increase sales. In essence these boil down to three areas of focus:

- Increasing the number of guests
- Increasing the average sale per guest (room rate + extras)
- Increasing the numbers of sales per guest (duration + number of visits)

  (These last two points contribute to the overall **lifetime value** of your guests – something we should always keep in mind when evaluating marketing activity.)

To increase the number of guests you need to know who your guests are, their needs, their expectations and their priorities. Then match these to what you are offering.

You need to stop thinking about **price** being your differentiator and start thinking about **value.** And in order to do this you have to understand what your perfect guest perceives as good value, and we'll start with this in **Chapter 1**.

And as it's not pricing you have to use to make you

stand out, in **Chapter 2** we'll help you identify what else can be your differentiator.

No doubt you already have a website, but how hard is your website working for you? Is it just a form of brochure, or does it actually help to attract potential guests and help the sales process? We'll explore the key principles of designing and maintaining your website(s) in **Chapter 3** to ensure maximum online visibility.

How well do you communicate with your guests to stimulate interest and most importantly some action? Whether online or offline, we'll cover key principles in **Chapter 4**.

We've already mentioned the need to focus on giving value, so we'll give you plenty of practical ideas to do this in **Chapter 5** to attract the attention of your guests and stimulate sales and return visits.

In **Chapter 6,** we'll discuss additional strategies for online marketing. It's easy to forget what we did before the advent of the Internet, so in **Chapter 7** we'll look at the traditional forms of marketing that still work today.

People are more likely to do business with, and remain loyal to, those they know, like and trust, so in **Chapter 8** we'll look at some of the strategies that help to build rapport, and help increase the lifetime value of every guest.

And however good you are, you can't do it all yourself, unless you plan to be there 24 hours a day and seven days a week. So **Chapter 9** looks at how to involve your team in converting potential guests into paying guests, increasing spend per head and helping to prompt future bookings to increase the lifetime value of every guest.

In **Chapter 10** we'll also discuss where and how you can get support from other businesses for mutual benefit, and find a source of potential guests.

You'll want to develop an overall strategy, and see how your actions affect your results. In **Chapter 11** we'll bring everything together, ensuring you have a plan that's easy for you to follow, to ensure you achieve **success** for **your hotel.**

This is what we'll help you achieve

- ✓ Tailor all your marketing to attract only the types of **guests you want,** who share your values and you love working with
- ✓ Identify what differentiates you from everyone else so you can shout about it and **stand out from your competition**
- ✓ Update your website and make use of social media to maximise your **online presence** to attract new business
- ✓ Write effective marketing copy that gets your **guests and prospects attention** – every time
- ✓ Tailor your services to add value and give

maximum perceived value for money to increase guests' spend per head and increase the **lifetime value** of every guest

- ✓ How to use **online marketing strategies** to raise your visibility and drive traffic to your website from other sources
- ✓ Make **cost effective** use of **traditional marketing** to work in tandem with online marketing activity
- ✓ **Build loyalty** from your guests so they keep coming back, and tell all their friends to come too
- ✓ Select the **right people,** and tell them everything they need to know to help you build your sales and profit
- ✓ Establish joint ventures to **collaborate** with suppliers, local businesses and even your competitors for a win – win
- ✓ Evaluate which marketing **strategies work for your business**, and which ones don't, so you don't waste your hard earned profits on ineffective marketing
- ✓ Draw up a longer-term **marketing plan** for the next 12 months

Knowledge is nothing without action! Throughout the book we recommend the actions you take to put everything into practice. These are indicated by this symbol

and the grey boxes. We recommend you download the complete exercises document from www.HotelSuccessHandbook.com

Personal objectives

Maybe not all of this is important to you right now, so you may find it useful to set your own objectives based on your own criteria for success; ones that are specific to **you** and your hotel. This can be helpful to give you some focus, and as you read through you'll be better able to pick up on the ideas relevant to **you**, **your** business, and **your** goals. Don't worry about making these too specific right now, we'll deal with specifics in Chapter 11.

Here are some examples:

- Increase profits to give more financial security
- Enjoy spending time with your guests
- Feel more confident about using the Internet as a marketing tool
- To increase occupancy at specific times to enable you to take a break at other times
- To be able to take a holiday knowing that your staff can handle things when you aren't there
- Identify the best marketing tactics to increase business

Action 0.1 Set your objectives

My criteria for success

What I want to learn or achieve as a result of this book

Make a plan

From now on, you will be gathering lots of ideas to implement in your business. Some of these will be quite long-term, and others you may be able to implement straight away. To make sure these ideas don't get lost, ensure you capture all the ones you feel are right for you.

It would be easy to just end up with a long list of things to do. There is nothing wrong with this – you can always come back and evaluate it afterwards. However, there may be ideas that strike a chord and you have some immediate thoughts on how they will work for you, so write them down.

We suggest these headings:

- Activity/action
- What this will achieve (which should relate to your original goals)
- How will you measure this (e.g. number of enquiries, number of actual bookings, total value of bookings/sales, total profit generated) Keep it simple enough that you can monitor the information
- What resources or help you will need, and what you could delegate
- When you want to achieve this by

Don't worry about completing every question for every idea you have – you can do this later. The point is to have a mechanism for recording as much as you can as you go. This will make it easier for you to review and prioritise when you come to finalise your plan.

Test and track everything

You won't want to throw away your hard-earned profits on marketing, promotions or training that does not deliver. **You need to test and track everything you do.**

To do this, you need to know where you started and start tracking from the outset. So record this on your plan, too.

Unless you set up the right measures, even when you can track your sales, you won't necessarily know what actions made the difference. So, for every advert people respond to you need to include a promotional code so that you can track which adverts have been most successful (see page 60 and Chapter 6). The same applies when people call – ask how them how they heard of you. Or – if they are regulars – find out if they are responding to a particular promotion, and where they saw it advertised. If you don't know what works and what doesn't, you won't know what to use in future, or where you are wasting your money.

Whenever you make changes to copy, track what impact this has on enquiries, the number of sales and the value of those sales.

Before you run a promotion, you need to know your sales and margin on the product or service you are promoting. Then measure the sales and margin while the promotion is running. Although you might have an uptake in sales, if your promotion means a lower margin, you may be worse off in terms of profit.

When you train your staff, check how effective the training has been. If you have set specific objectives, this make your training easier to measure, but it's impossible if you don't know what improvements you are looking for.

Treat any spend on increasing sales as an investment; not a cost. Any investment you make **must** give you a return. If not, analyse how you can improve on it, and either make changes or stop doing it altogether.

Action 0. 2 Plan template

Now draw up your Plan template – it's up to you whether you do this on your computer, or on paper. Whichever it is, have it in a format that you can add to and update every time you have another idea. Don't worry about having too much on it at this stage – we will help you to prioritise it all at the end of the book.

You can download an Excel template from our website www.HotelSuccessHandbook.com

Chapter 1

Who are your guests and what are you selling?

Chapter 1

Who are your guests and what are you selling?

First things first – before you invest a single penny or spend any of your valuable time on marketing and increasing sales, you need to identify three things:

> Who are your guests? (More specifically – who are your **perfect** guests?)
>
> What are you offering them?
>
> What makes you different?

These three answers will provide the cornerstones to how you increase your occupancy levels, spend per head, and – ultimately – your profit.

Knowing more about your guests, what they want and what you can offer to meet these wants means that:

- ✓ You can make sure you target all your benefits at your guests
- ✓ All your 'advertised' answers are to problems you know your guests would like to have solved
- ✓ Your prices are right for your target guests (they perceive they are getting good value for money)
- ✓ Your service is of (or above) the standard your

guests expect

- ✓ You can offer packages and incentives that relate to your guests' attitudes and interests
- ✓ You can set your USP (unique selling proposition) to appeal directly to your target market – either creating an affinity with them or demonstrating that you know exactly what they want
- ✓ You can position your 'brand' correctly, so that it appeals to your guests. (By brand we mean your whole image, and what you represent to your guests, the way your staff interact with guests, and the way you communicate).

You need to have a 'picture' of your ideal guests in mind **every time** you start any marketing activity for your business. If it helps, literally create a mental picture of your customer or guests and imagine them receiving or responding to the web page, offer, letter, advert or phone call you are thinking about. In this chapter we will focus on the first two questions (who are your guests? and what are you offering them?), and in Chapter 2 we'll concentrate on what makes you different, so you stand out from your competition.

Identify your perfect guest

The best place to start to get more guests into your hotel is to really understand who your guest is and what needs you are satisfying when they buy from you. In everything you do to market your business, think about your guest (and remember, you are not them).

Too many places try to appeal to everyone and end up satisfying no one. This doesn't mean to say that you won't have more than one type of guest; for example, you may focus on business users during the week but still be a perfect destination for a romantic weekend break. But just consider the compatibility of your two or three main target markets.

Take a good look at your guests

You may already attract only the guests you want, all the time; but for now, let's assume you're not. Even if you are now, this could change.

The first thing to ask is: do you know who your guests are? Not just by name, but a very clear picture of the **type** of people you want as guests. Are you hoping to attract...

- Families with young children who may be visiting local attractions?
- Business people looking for a home from home and somewhere to unwind?
- Couples for a romantic weekend break?
- Young water sport fanatics?
- Families needing a bed for the night whilst visiting friends or relatives?
- Wedding parties?
- People who enjoy the outdoors?

- Business conferences and events?
- Overseas visitors to see historical and cultural attractions?
- People on shopping sprees?
- Locals to drink in the bar or eat in your restaurant?

Whichever category it is, be very clear about who your guests are.

Now write down all the attributes of your perfect guests. Here's a checklist for you:

- Their likes and dislikes
- Their budget
- Their perceptions of value for money (not the same as their budget)
- What they define as good service
- How often they visit your area
- How often they take a holiday
- Who they travel with
- Their interests and hobbies
- Where else they travel to
- How they spend their time away from the hotel
- How they like to travel
- How old they are
- What they do with their time whilst in the hotel
- Where they like to eat

- Their favourite foods
- What they like to eat (not necessarily their favourite food all of the time)
- Their values
- What 'demographic' they are (e.g. young urban couples, middle income families with children)
- What influences their decisions
    - **logic,** e.g. cost and practicalities, or
    - **emotion**, look, image and gut feel
- Their birthday and other special occasion dates

Now go back and check the list again, answering **only** where you can verify claims with questionnaires, independent research, comments from guests, and feedback – **not** what you **think** your guests would say.

If you try to improve the results of your hotel based on what **you think** your guests want, you could get it wrong. There is only **one way** to really know what your guests want and that is to **ask them** and get their opinion.

It is important to go through your list again and **only** tick those categories and fill in the details where you can substantiate your claim with real feedback and information that your guests have provided. Second-guessing will not get you the results you want; it's as simple as that. In this case, for sure, the 'customer knows best'.

Establish a demand

Analyse which guests currently are your most profitable. Also remember that unless you are in business only to meet new people, any market you consider has to be profitable. So if you are considering new categories of guests that are not currently your most profitable, do your sums first; do they have the income or budget to pay the prices you need to charge to make a healthy profit?

This does change. Beware a market that is already saturated or declining; if the market is not there, no amount of promotion on your part is going to magically attract these people back. Many hotels are finding the business market declining, and if this is the case for you, ask yourself: Should I be focusing on a different market, or on the same market but a different offer?

Check your compatibility

Once you've identified a potential niche, consider whether or not these are the type of guests you would really want to be attracting more of to your hotel – they may be very profitable, but do you really want to be working with this type of guest all of the time? How satisfying would it be for you to be focusing more of your time and effort into servicing these people?

If your target market doesn't excite you, your work will be unrewarding, and it will have a knock-on effect on the perceived level of service you provide. It's very important to find a balance of profit and guest types you are happy with.

Action 1.1 Describe your perfect guest

Don't worry if these are not the type of guests you have now. Look back at all the questions above and give as much detail as possible.

Now put all of this together to paint the picture of your perfect guest, and keep this image in your mind with any activity you do to:

- generate **more guests**;
- make them visit you **more often**;
- get **more sales**; and
- make **more profit**.

Understand your guests' needs and expectations

You will never be able to market effectively to your guests unless you really know who they are and what's important to them. From now on, look at everything from your guests' perspective. We can't emphasise this enough – you really do need to understand what they want or what they expect when they come and stay with you. We'll say it again... it's not about what you think your guests want, it's what they actually want.

Identify your guests' highest priorities. What are

the things that they are prepared to pay a premium for? What criteria do they use to assess these? For example, if value for money is important, what factors do they consider when determining value for money? What are the things that are of high value to them but low cost to you, which you can then use to get their attention?

All these factors influence the ways in which you attract more business and retain existing guests. So you need to know **who** your guests are before you can work out **where** to find them.

And – if you **really** want to understand your guests – you **must ask them.**

Action 1.2 What are your guests' needs and expectations?

What are their highest priorities?

What are the things they are likely to pay a premium for?

What criteria do they use to assess these?

Identify your 'buyer'

Your buyer and your guest are not necessarily one and the same person. Let us explain. All the people who actually come and stay in your hotel may not always be the same as the people making the booking (although in most leisure cases one of the party is). The people making the booking or doing the initial research may be somebody quite different or they may be just one of the party and not representative of the whole group. You need to think about this – they could be working to a 'brief' or their own ideals...

Here are some examples to get you thinking about who are your 'bookers' and who are your 'guests':

If your target market is families with children, the likelihood is that it will be Mum doing the research and making the booking. She is most likely going to have all her requirements in mind for making sure the kids are looked after. You will probably also need to appeal to the influential 10-year-old, or the demands a toddler might present! And Dad will want to make sure he can enjoy himself, too...

If you're trying to capture the business market, will it be the boss or his/her personal assistant (PA) who makes the decision where they eat or stay? What grabs their attention? They may use very different criteria from the person actually staying or eating with you. If you're getting a lot of bookings through PAs for example, make sure you're clearly explaining your 'key features' as they will probably be working to a brief and being less swayed by 'emotion' when booking.

So, your next task is to find out (if you don't already know) **who** is making the enquiries and bookings and see if they are a different person or market to your guests.

 Action 1.3 Who are your buyers?

For one week make a note of all the people making your bookings (or if you already know this information, look back over your recent bookings).

Keep a tally of all your bookings, whether or not the 'buyer' is one of the party, and, if not, what their role is e.g. travel agent, PA, relative, club secretary

Now for each group track back over Exercises 1.1 and 1.2 and complete the same exercises for your 'buyers' – you need to know how they think too.

For all future exercises keep this 'booker' group in mind, too.

What are you really selling?

You might think this is a stupid question – you obviously sell a hotel room or a holiday or a conference facility or whatever else your guests buy from you. But you need to be more specific about 'what it is' to focus your marketing messages and business objectives.

Once you know your guest, it's a lot easier to think about how you describe what you are offering to them. So when guests come to you, you are not just providing a hotel room or a meal; it's a solution to their problem or an experience they want.

Physical description

First, decide what you sell physically and make a list of what describes it. Start to think about specifics in terms of location, features, who it's for and how you deliver these.

So if you're a hotel in Bournemouth, for example, focusing on the leisure market, here's what you might list:

- Short breaks
- Summer holidays
- Winter holidays
- Weekends away
- UK holidays
- Family holidays
- Beach holidays
- Shopping holidays
- Holidays within two hours of London
- Affordable luxury hotel rooms
- Personal service for a special stay
- Unique 1920s hotel building

But for the same hotel, if you want to attract business users, it would be more appropriate to list:

- A relaxing environment to run a workshop
- A place to focus before an important meeting
- Easily accessible meeting location

- Private business briefing breakfast
- Full support of a fully equipped business centre
- Convenience of late check in
- On-tap refreshment facilities

Now start to **put some of these descriptions of what you sell together** and you'll have started to define what it is that you physically sell:

> *"Year-round affordable luxury UK beachside family holidays within 2 hours of London with personal service in a unique 1920s building."*

Emotional description

Now think about what it is that you sell as an **emotion** or **experience.** This will also help you to define what you are selling and whom you are selling it to.

Considering again the example of a hotel in Bournemouth, this could be:

Leisure

- Relaxing views of the sea
- Sanctuary within two hours of London
- An affordable escape any time of year
- A environmentally conscience-easing break you can travel to by train
- Somewhere entertaining to spend time as a family

- A place where there are no demands on you or your time

Business

- Hassle-free conference facilities
- Home from home for regular business travellers
- Somewhere to truly unwind after a busy day
- Minimum fuss 'express' lunch service.

So you might say:

> *"Your home from home, somewhere to relax and unwind at the end of your busy working day."*

Now you can add this to your physical description and understand what it is that you are **really** selling – which isn't just a room in a hotel.

Results description

The final stage is to focus on what you do for the guest.

Use phases such as '...so that you (can)...'

Leisure

- Truly relax and unwind
- Have some time for yourself
- Don't have to worry about what to do with the kids this summer
- Don't have to worry if the weather's not so

good

- Have all your entertainment right on your doorstep

Business

- Focus on your business meeting
- Get a good night's sleep and be refreshed for your busy day ahead
- Be reassured you can still get something to eat before you leave
- Conduct your business in total privacy
- Not waste a minute of your busy day
- Brief your team in private before your clients arrive
- Save yourself valuable time

Putting the descriptions together

Putting physical, emotional and results descriptions together, we can see how they work in context. Here are two examples:

Example 1

Let's imagine the businesswoman who is coming to stay with you for one night because she's attending a meeting in your town the next day. She wants a **solution to the problem** of finding somewhere to stay that is clean, comfortable and feels secure; will accommodate a late check in to fit in with her travel arrangements. She probably wants a meal sitting somewhere where she won't feel vulnerable sitting on her own. And Internet access from her room. She's also looking for somewhere where she can get a good night's sleep, have a quick breakfast and check out with minimum fuss.

You say:

> *"Friendly, secure and comfortable hotel, easy to find in the centre of town with ample free parking (also easy to reach by train). Our business travel package includes Wi-Fi connection, in- room dining or a meal in our relaxed bistro, late check- in and early breakfast available (in your room at no extra charge if requested). We also provide our uniquely blended essential bath oil to help you de-stress. Then have a great night's sleep in one of our double rooms at single prices on luxury xyz beds (we're the only hotel in the county to offer them!), and check out online from the comfort of your room if you want to – just hand over the keys when you leave."*

Example 2

For the couple on a weekend break, coming to you for **an experience** – getting away from their hectic city lives to the tranquillity of the countryside; the cosiness of the lounge with an open fire; the luxury of the spa; the indulgence of the fantastic food; and a welcome chance of a long lie in and breakfast in bed.

You say:

> *"An easy and picturesque two-hour drive from*

London (we'll send you detailed directions for our favourite routes). You can arrive in time for complimentary afternoon tea with our special recipe homemade cakes, scones and locally produced jam. Then relax before dinner cooked by our award-winning chef, take a walk in our privately owned 40-acre estate, or enjoy a signature spa treatment we can book for you in advance (we're the only hotel in the south of England to offer abc treatments).

Even for one-night stays we offer a late check-out of 12 midday, giving you time to enjoy breakfast in bed (at no extra charge) or stay in bed until it's time to get up and enjoy our renowned brunch (served until 1pm on weekends)."

In Action 1.4, identify what needs you are satisfying for **your** ideal guests (based on their feedback and requests) and look at everything from their perspective.

Go on – put your ideas together (and don't worry if none of your brochures or your website say this at the moment – that's what we're going to be working on getting right!). **Ignore** all your current marketing messages and those of your competitors. Really write down what it is that your hotel **offers** and what **your guests say about it**.

Remember to think about what you do as a business, not just as a list of facts and features but emotions and experiences.

Combine these to explain what you offer. Use your guest feedback and quotes in this exercise – it's not all about what **you** think. You need to include what **guests** think; as it's them you are selling to.

Action 1.4 Identify the needs you satisfy for your ideal guests

What needs do you satisfy for your ideal guest?
What are you selling?
Put the physical, emotional and results descriptions together
What does this do or how does this help your guests?

Chapter 1 recap

By now you've established your target audience, and what it is you are actually offering, you are in a much stronger position to shape your marketing and sales process to appeal to your **perfect guest**. Everything else you do as a result of this book should be done with your perfect guest as the focus.

So in summary, always keep in mind:

- ✓ Your perfect guest(s) – who they are, what's important to them when they book and stay in a hotel, what they like/dislike, their needs and expectations
- ✓ Who else makes bookings on behalf of your

guests, and what appeals to them

✓ What (in detail) you are offering your guests physically, emotionally and how, so you can get their attention

Authors' comments

Caroline: I can always tell a hotel or restaurant that is trying to please everyone, as they are not focused and consistent with their messages and training. The difference is measurable when we work towards a niche market. I've seen this in my own business, too, where once I recognised I had to really focus on the type of businesses I wanted to work with, the way I attracted clients was always done with my ideal in mind. I certainly would not have written this book if I were still marketing at 'any' business.

Lucy: When I work with businesses that have a very clear idea of who their customers are, it's **much** easier to get great results from marketing and promotional campaigns. You know who the website is designed for; you know the language to use and the benefits to focus on. You want to set your self apart from the competition and be different but this also **has** to appeal to your ideal guests so if you don't know who they are you're a bit stuck!

Please don't read and act on the rest of this book until you've got a very clear picture of who your perfect hotel guest is, as the results will never be as good if you don't.

Chapter 2

What's different about you?

Chapter 2

What's different about you?

Now that you have worked out your perfect guest and what's important to them (and also know the 'booker'), you can really define all the differences in your service and accommodation that will make your unique selling proposition (USP) more appealing than your competition.

Don't just end up being the same as everyone else. Every hotel has something that makes it unique. What do **you** give that will make you stand out from the crowd? Why should anyone choose to stay with you rather than any of your competitors?

In this chapter we will help you to:

- ✓ Identify how you compare with your competition so you can pick out the factors that make you different
- ✓ Find ways of incorporating your passions and values into your business so you can attract the type of guests who share these, and you'll love working with
- ✓ Plan your marketing messages around an 'expert' topic, to capture your guests' interest
- ✓ Define your identity and position your 'brand' well, so that it appeals to your guests.
- ✓ Identify your USP (Unique Selling Proposition) to appeal directly to your target market

Assess your competition

To identify what you can do that's different, you need to **assess your competition.**

Who else is competing for your perfect guest? Get out there and see for yourself what they are doing. If other hotels in your town or street, or area are offering a similar theme, the same deals, or identical style of service, you need to change something that gives you an edge. Even if you were doing it first and they've copied you, what can you now do to make what **you** do different, but still being true to your identity?

Bear in mind your competition may not be just other hotels. If your main market is family holidays, you will be competing with alternative holiday destinations either at home or abroad; if you cater for weddings you may be competing with exotic beach locations and if you offer business-meeting facilities you may well be competing with a company's own in-house facilities.

Think about what it is that gives you an advantage; is it your location, garden and fantastic views, is it peace, tranquillity and intimacy, is it sheer luxury and indulgence, or is it fantastic food, made from locally sourced organic foods, lovingly prepared by your award-winning chef?

Before answering any of these, ask yourself what is it that your guests find appealing; it's not what you think that counts; it's what **they** think. And if you don't know the answer to this question – **ask**.

After assessing the competition you might also identify where there is a gap in the market; something that your guests want that no one else is offering; something new that you could offer that you don't already.

Write up what it is that you **really** offer. And make sure there are **personal** and **unique** touches that mean no other hotel could use your words. And if you think you don't have anything unique...

- What about the **people** in your business? Your chef is unique, and you or your hotel manager are unique to your business. Think about personalities and what they bring. Anything your chef makes to his or her own recipe is different. Anything that you or your manager have 'hand-picked' or 'make a rule about' is unique to you. Talk about it in your marketing messages.
- Or if you need a 'quick win' unique feature – think about **services, features or facilities** you can add that are unique in your town/area/hotel market. Being the only provider with a certain brand of toiletry/spa treatment/linen/access to event or special access/recipe/early or late service, or offer can make you different. Be creative – it doesn't need to be expensive but **must** be in keeping with your ideal guests' preferences and likes. If they are eco–conscious, do something green, if they are obsessed with 'value' include something that offers exceptional value for money (see Chapter 5).

You do need to be different to your competitors to

attract guests. But different does not necessarily mean 'better' or 'cheaper' or 'bigger' or 'more established' or any other preconception you may have that you can't compete with.

There needs to be at least one thing that you do that is different **and** appeals to your perfect guest.

Being different can be as simple as:

- Having a different 'look' to your **website** (it may be the design of your photo gallery or that your website is written in the style of a blog or uses lots of video, for example). All this will communicate your personality and style which you can align with your ideal guests (modern, or traditional, information rich, or design led for example
- Featuring **you** and/or **your staff** widely in your marketing (you are all unique individuals so there is no way anyone can 'copy' your views, opinions, mannerisms and styles)
- Offering a **type of accommodation** that isn't available in your area – yurts, log cabins, group and family rooms, for example
- Offering different **activities**, such as a croquet lawn, bird-watching hides, adventure team building exercises, treasure hunts, tours in vintage cars
- Your **look and feel** – think about your handmade items, your décor, the building itself, the views and location
- Handling **initial enquiries** – can you be

different? Make your website and brochures different, send a postcard, produce short videos? You can do a lot to differentiate yourself from the competition. Again if it's just that you feature you or your staff in your marketing it's already different.

- Your **food and drinks**, and other services you offer – anything that you can do differently that cannot be copied as it's unique to your chef or bar. What about offering:
    - **hand-cooked snacks and local wine** on arrival if you are catering for foodies
    - the widest and best selection of quality **wines by the glass** for guests and locals alike
- Offering **office services** for business users or access to a PA/VA
- Provide **novelty items** in your rooms, such as fun slippers and bathrobes if you're focusing on couples.
- Offer an unusual setting for **wedding photos**, even for the wettest day (some great artwork or feature wallpaper in a public area may be all you need to do this for example).
- Making **you and your staff more prominent** in your business. People like to buy from people – by promoting yourselves you can instantly attach personality and uniqueness to what you offer.

Think about everything you are doing with your hotel and your marketing and ask yourself – is this something different? Can I make it appear 'unique'? Will it appeal directly to my perfect guests? Then ask yourself – Is this something I am comfortable about delivering? It still **must** sit within your identity and within your capabilities.

Now you need to work out which attributes you can **add** to, to make them **unique statements** that only your hotel can use.

There will be unique **combinations** of features and benefits that you offer, and that's the key. For example, you will be one of many hotels by the sea, and one of many hotels offering theatre and wine lovers weekends, but you might be the only one offering a combination of the two.

If you are struggling with this, read on to the end of the chapter, as it might spark some more ideas. Then come back here and have another go at this exercise. Having something different to say is going to make marketing and promoting your hotel much easier so don't think this isn't important!

Action 2.1 How are you different?

Write up a list of your attributes and all the things you do or offer – anything that relates to the hotel itself, your guests' stay, or their overall experience:

Features

The accommodation

Your location

Activities

You

Your team

Your menu

Your bar and wine selection

What you provide in your rooms

Your function packages

Now go back over this list and identify:

The things that are generic and can be applied to any hotels in your area or sector

The things that are already different, or that with a little effort could be made into something different

What attributes or offerings can you combine to make you appear unique?

Now summarise the things you could confidently promote as being different and 'unique' to your hotel.

Be passionate about your business

Everything you've identified about your perfect guest and your offer should really excite you. If it doesn't you might want to think again. When you considered who your perfect guest was, you were bound to have been influenced by your own priorities, your own values and your own likes and dislikes.

Take this a step further and imagine your perfect

guest sharing some of the same passions and values as you. It's a lot easier to market and sell something that you are passionate about or that's important to you.

If you don't love what you do, or feel it's important, it will show. It will be very hard for you to deliver a good service if you are dealing with people with whom you share no values, interests or enthusiasm.

So start by listing what you enjoy, what you are passionate about, and what's important to you. Can these be incorporated into your business? If your business reflects your interests, the likelihood is you'll attract other people who share them. You are more likely to be able to build rapport with them, and you can be more targeted (and successful) with your marketing, both externally and on-site.

Create your values around what is **important to you**. If it's important to you to only use fresh, local ingredients when available, or to use sustainable resources, or care for the environment, create your values around these principles. Make sure your staff understand these values, too. Then show your guests how you incorporate these into your business. If you can't live up to them, think again.

If what you are passionate about is what you are already selling – **make that clear**. Maybe you've positioned all the baths in your hotel so that they have a view; or you only use organic sausages from the award-winning butcher in your town for breakfasts; or you only use a certain hire car company as they provide free sat-nav – or whatever it is that you think about, **share this detail**.

If you love:

- **Golf**, you'll find it easy to research (that's the good bit!), promote and sell golfing with your holidays or business packages (and maybe negotiate preferential green fees with your local courses)
- **Gardening**, write up a guide to all the local gardens to visit in your area and perhaps hold a tour of your own hotel gardens
- **Dogs** (and they are allowed to stay), write a guide to the 10 best dog walks from your hotel
- **Shopping**, write a guide to your local shops and negotiate some discount vouchers with traders
- **Food**, write your own reviews and feature other people's reviews in a 'where to eat guide'
- **Keeping fit**, describe the best running routes, sports facilities and places to hire sports equipment
- **Cooking**, open up your kitchen or offer cooking courses on your holidays either at your accommodation or nearby

And if you value:

- **Supporting your local community**, explain how you source local produce whenever possible (and what you consider constitutes 'local'), the measures you take to recruit local people, and the activities you are involved in to support local charities, projects or organisations

- **Being in the countryside,** describe your local walks, the type of wildlife guests might see, the views and the peace and quiet your guest will experience
- **Energy conservation**, give examples of the steps you have made to reduce your energy consumption, the systems you've implemented or equipment installed, and training you give staff to save energy
- **Fair trade**, talk about the products you now use and where they come from, or the changes you have made in your purchasing and vetting of suppliers to support this

And **share all this in advance**.

Your prospective guests need to know that you have these passions and offer these services and advice **before** they make the decision to come and stay.

If your passion appeals to your perfect guests, it will make your job of marketing your hotel and making it unique so much easier.

Think about every aspect of the experience you sell and how you can make it unique and aligned to your passions:

- What can **you** or your staff write that will be a unique guide or report?
- What is nearby (attractions, amenities, your location) that you enjoy and that makes you

unique?

- Think about transport. Can you offer a different way for people to arrive, depart or travel while they are staying with you? Vintage cars, motorbikes, horses, quads, snow shoes?
- What's your hobby? Could you set up holidays or recreational activities or even business activities for people who share this hobby?

Here's an example of where passions have shaped a businesss:

The **Running Inn** was a B&B in Eastbourne owned and run by two fitness trainers and expert runners. It operated as a B&B and hosted fitness and running weekends, making it different from every other B&B in Eastbourne. This way its competition was not just 'where shall I stay in Eastbourne' but it competed nationally for 'where shall I go for a fitness or running training weekend?' (With no location specified). Owners Mike and Fiona got to fill their B&B with lots of 'perfect guests' who were like-minded about fitness (although not all their guests are as fit as they are – Lucy can personally vouch for that!). *Mike & Fiona have now sold the guesthouse and run fitness weekends with the new owners, and other local hotels as 'The Running Inn'.*

This is a perfect example of turning your passion into the type of holidays that you want and attracting your perfect guests.

Another example of this might be Rick Stein – his hotels and holiday accommodation in Padstow are an extension of his restaurants and cooking school, and reflect his love for the local area and its produce. You **come** for the food (Rick's passion) but you **stay** to enjoy the location.

Your passion should already influence what you offer – and if it doesn't, you need to reconsider what you are doing. Whether you focus on just one of your passions, or a number of passions, it's the combination of these that add up to make **your** hotel different. You'll find it easy to share detail and communicate your real passions which will not only make your hotel seem unique, but attract like-minded guests.

Action 2.2 What are your passions and values?

Write a list of things you enjoy doing or are interested in or passionate about (list anything you do and believe in both in 'work' and 'play').

What are the things you value most?

Which of these can be reflected in your business, and how?

Become an expert

One way of really capitalising on your interests and capturing the interest of your guests or prospects is to become an 'expert' in something that they (and you) are interested in.

Becoming an expert gives your hotel something that will make you stand out from everyone else. It also means you are more likely to attract the type of guests with whom you can build up a good rapport and a better prospect of repeat business. It's very easy to be enthusiastic and passionate about something that interests you, and this enthusiasm will translate into bookings if managed smartly.

An expert topic gives you the opportunity to get noticed by writing articles, blog posts, guidebooks or maybe even organising clubs or seminars in your hotel relevant to the topic. Any of these expert-related actions can form great PR and an opportunity to attract the attention of your prospects, and are also a fantastic way to help you build your prospect list. They enquire or request information and in return you get their contact details

Here are a few examples of how you can use your expertise to get guests:

- If you have a **spa**, you could write articles about different treatments and therapies, and put together your own small guide.
- If your hotel is popular with **golfers**, you could include tips from a golf pro, blog about golf tournaments, or review local courses.
- If you have an interest in **classic cars**, you might want to promote classic car events in the area, write about the events, and maybe even chart your progress with your own car if you have one.

- If you have a particularly extensive or unusual **wine list** and want to make this a feature, you could review the wines, or ask your wine supplier to write articles for you.
- If you have an unusual or particularly renowned menu, using local ingredients, put together your own **recipe book**. You may even want to include the source of some of your ingredients and maybe get your key suppliers to share the costs. Then offer cookery lessons or courses centred on your signature dishes.

All these examples are ways of being **unique** and **different** using your expertise. You can make your expertise the differentiating factor of your hotel, and a way of connecting with a potential audience. If you have a very niche interest, then this will translate to a very niche target market, so try and have a focused but broad enough area of expertise.

Having a specific area of expertise also makes it easier for you to find a forum or networking group where you can get your name known, as well as finding potential opportunities and prospective joint ventures (see Chapter 10). And once established as an expert, you can build on this by offering themed events and weekends.

One word of warning on your expert topic – don't let this detract from the basics of a well-run hotel. Get the basics right first – your accommodation, service and food – then focus on your areas of special interest. No use having the best-run spa in the county if your rooms don't live up to it, and you certainly won't attract wine lovers if your food isn't up to the same quality as the wine, for example.

Action 2.3 List your interests

List your interests, hobbies or any topics which you have enough first hand knowledge to be an expert in

How could you develop this expertise to incorporate it into your hotel?

What could you write about or do to get initial attention as an expert?

What other opportunities are there for activities and events based around your expert topic?

Who else might you work with to develop or deliver this special expert topic?

Define your identity (set out your brand)

Now you know to whom you are selling, what you are selling and what you do that's different, your identity is next on the list for attention.

Your identity is more than just a logo, or a photo of your hotel. Your identity or 'brand' should encompass your values, show how you want to be perceived and reflect your personality. Ensure your identity is compatible with your target market; is it something that will engage, inspire, and attract the type of guests you want, not the ones you don't?

If your identity portrays a professional, businesslike, no-nonsense service, where discretion and efficiency are your number one values, this will not be a good match if your target market is young families. And what will appeal to young families probably won't appeal to the business user. So create a set of brand values or promises that your guests care about. It's not enough to just 'decide' you are going to target a certain market – you need to 'look the part' too.

It's not just the 'words' but the 'pictures' and the 'actions' you take that also convey your identity and brand. You can't just say one thing and 'be' another.

And you must avoid following the herd. Focus on what makes your hotel different and how that's better for your guests. Focus on your strengths and what you're most proud of to help you define your niche and your identity.

To get you thinking about your identity or brand values compare yourself to some famous brands. For example, if you were a car, what make would you be; if a supermarket, what brand would you be; if a clothes shop, which one? Reflecting on your responses, what are the key things that define each of these brands, and are these values that you want to reflect in your own business?

Action 2.4 What is your identity?

What are the key factors you want to reflect in the identity of your hotel?

What are the things you value most?

How would you sum up the personality of you, your team, and the hotel as a whole?

What is the look and image you most reflect?

What feelings and emotions do you conjure up? (e.g. relaxation, excitement, security, peace of mind, entertainment)

Be consistent

You must be consistent with the identity you portray. Choose colours, images and words in all your marketing that reflect your personality as a brand, and ensure that your services, decor, food offer, and staff are all congruent with your identity.

This doesn't mean all your rooms have to be the same colours as you use in your logo (we're joking a little now!), but it's very important to understand that actions and the real experience along with your 'words and pictures' define who you are. Sometimes you'll hear this referred to as 'posture' – and it's the same concept as making sure your outfit matches a dress code for an occasion.

Set criteria to ensure this consistency, and put in

place processes and procedures, and train your team to ensure your values are always reflected in everything you do.

There is little point investing time, effort and money into perfecting your marketing and sales processes if the experience does not match what you're promoting.

Your identity is only as good as what you portray to your guests, so ask for feedback to check that the image you intend to convey sends the right message. Be prepared to adapt or change accordingly.

Action 2.5 Sum up your identity

How would you now sum up your identity? Pick out your key words from Action 2.4

What is the overall theme?

Now sum up your image in one sentence

What look, colours, words and images will convey this image?

What's your story?

You have decided who your perfect guest is. They probably reflect the type of people you want to spend time with, work with or have as guests because you have an affinity with them, share a passion, or like to engage with them.

And we've already established that you need to communicate to your guests what is different about your hotel, about what it is that gives you that edge. And we've discussed the need to be consistent with the message and image you convey. Now it's time to bring it all together in **your hotel's story**.

This is your chance to show why you are perfect for your ideal guests. This is the point where you make sure you tell everyone about and demonstrate your difference – **in detail**.

Describe what you do, who you are, what is important to you, what makes your hotel different, what makes you the best in your market or your area or your price range. And don't be afraid to go into detail – make it interesting, **tell a story**. The more detail you give, the more compelling the offer – providing it meets your ideal guests' needs.

Here are some more examples of being different and how telling a story can help.

If all your meat comes from a local **organic farm**, describe this, maybe even a little bit about the farm; how you choose your meat and what makes it so delicious. Even go so far as having photos of the pigs running around! Seriously. People love detail if it's what appeals to them.

If you've made efforts to reduce your **carbon footprint,** detail your goals, what steps you've taken so far, the support you've had, the changes you've made to your systems, purchasing, equipment, and training. Tell them about the quirky practices or products you are using, and what guests might see around the hotel as part of your mission. What has been the impact to date, and what are your plans for the future?

If you provide a **picnic lunch**, make sure you tell people not only that you provide them, but go into detail about what's included, about the quality of the products, and about how it can make their day special, and what opportunities it opens for their day out. Give some example itineraries, places to go, discount vouchers – the ideal 'morning for walkers' or an 'afternoon out for foodies'. Don't just end up being the same as everyone else. It only makes your job harder.

If you've designed all your **rooms around a particular theme**, tell them how this came about, the research you did, the features you've incorporated and the added extras they can expect in their chosen room to add interest. If you've had a checklist or criteria for your rooms then share this with guests. It's not to brag, but to show the care, thoroughness and attention that you've given to their experience.

You know that even if you're in a road with 20 other hotels, there will be unique personalities in your business or values that you can promote.

Now it's time to tell your guests about your special features and **in detail** to ensure they book with **you** and not your competitors. Keep your perfect guest(s) in mind throughout, and show you really understand them.

 Action 2.6 What's your story?

Now bring everything together from all the Actions in this chapter remembering your ideal guests. Write up your story to include: what you are selling which is unique, what makes you different, and your passions and values to reflect your identity.

Chapter 2 recap

By now you've established what makes you 'unique' so you can differentiate yourself and stand out from your competition.

So in summary, always keep in mind:

- ✓ How you are different from everyone else so you can shout about it and stand out from your competition
- ✓ What are your passions and values, and how these can be reflected in your business to attract guests who share these
- ✓ What you could establish as your expert topic
- ✓ Your identity, and how you can ensure a consistent message to reflect this

Authors' comments

Caroline: I've worked too often with clients who really have no affinity with their guests. And it tends to show the minute you walk through the door. Guests pick up these vibes, too. If this is you, maybe it's time for a rethink on your ideal guest.

Lucy: Putting yourself 'out there' may be uncomfortable at first, but it really does make a huge difference to your business. People still like to buy from people even in this increasingly 'online' world – and the reason your guests want to stay with you and not a chain/corporate hotel is that personality is obviously important to them. This is no time for you or your team to be shrinking violets – but do what's comfortable for you, and your hotel will benefit enormously.

Chapter 3

Review your website

Chapter 3

Review your website

Your hotel website is important to your business success. However, a website is not a 'finished piece' of marketing, and you need to update and edit it constantly – so it can always be working its hardest for you.

In this chapter, we'll show you how to:

✓ Take control of your website so that you can keep it up-to-date and focused

✓ Make sure that you've included everything your guests and prospects need to know – and that it's clear where to find answers

✓ Make good use of photos and videos

✓ Maximise your online visibility

Manage your own content

If you don't already have a website that allows <u>you</u> – not your design company or website agency – to update, edit and make changes to your site easily, now is the time to seriously consider this.

If you need to go back to your designer or website agency every time you want to make an edit, add a page, set up an offer – or really do anything on your website – you need to have a great relationship with them, and they must be quick to respond. Or seriously consider changing your website to a system you can access yourself.

A **content management system** (a CMS) describes a website where you can access and edit design and content of your website online, at any time.

Many agencies sell their own CMS or use one that's already been written. These don't have to be expensive, and the time and costs you save in the long run can be immense.

For example, in her website design business, Lucy uses the free blog software WordPress to power websites like a CMS for many clients. She also recommends other CMS systems that are specifically written for hotels and other holiday companies that manage online bookings.

Being able to respond and adapt your website will always help your hotel business succeed. Your website is central to your marketing and promotions – it's your 24-hour brochure and salesperson, so it needs to bring you guests.

What's the purpose of your website?

Your immediate answer might be:

> *"to promote my hotel and get bookings".*

It **is** there to promote your hotel and get bookings – but is that all? And does it have **all** the information a prospective guest needs to make a booking?

The objectives of your website should be clear, and you need to think about them **all** the time you are working on your website.

So what do you want your website to achieve? Here are some ideas:

- Showcase your hotel
- Explain why your hotel is different to the competition
- Take bookings online
- Generate phone enquires
- Share availability information – saving you and your staff time with enquiries
- Promote special offers and packages
- Sell your location and surrounding area – promote your 'destination'
- Describe the type of stays, holidays, events and experiences people can have staying with you – and their benefits
- Demonstrate your value for money (this is not

the same as low prices – it's how you explain the level of your prices – even if they are high)

- Promote your expertise as a hotel/restaurant/location in providing the perfect holiday/venue/stay/event.

Action 3.1 Write the business objectives for your website

Write down everything that's important to your business, especially those things that make you **different** and **unique.**

Have the list ready to reference when we work through all the actions to improve your website.

Measure your website traffic

If you already have a website, take a look at your analytics. (If you don't have analytics set up measuring your website traffic already, stop everything now and do this – there's no point even adjusting anything on your website if you can't measure its impact).

Google provides a free analytics package and this is good enough to show you the key information about how your website is working, and where traffic is coming from. To set up Google Analytics on your website (if you don't already have it) you just need to sign up and get your own 'code' to add to the back end of your website. You can then login online to your Google account and access your analytics.

As with any marketing and sales activity, you need to know what is and isn't working. By understanding how, when, what and why visitors are coming to your website, you can make it work harder (or keep doing more of what is already working).

With website analytics you can find out:

- Which keywords are people typing into search engines to reach your site
- What information people are reading on your site (the pages they look at)
- Which websites are pushing traffic to you
- How many enquiries you get a day/week/month
- How many enquiries you convert into sales

With Google Analytics you can also set up 'goals' on your website to measure specific actions – this could be as straightforward as the number of enquiry forms completed (so you get a traffic to  enquiry ratio). Other goals on your website could be downloading a mini brochure, call me request, email form completion, getting to the pricing page – whatever will help you understand if your website is working or not.

If you're serious about making your website work harder, and contribute to your hotel's success, you must have a way of measuring this. Analytics is your website success yardstick and you should be looking at the results every day.

Action 3.2 Make use of analytics

If you haven't done so already, set up Analytics on your website.

If you already have Analytics – take a fresh look and make note of your findings (look at keywords, referring sites, pages visited, enquiries made). Get familiar with what Analytics can show you about your website.

Set up goals on your Analytics that fit with your website objectives (e.g. enquiries, bookings, downloading a brochure).

Explain everything!

A big mistake that people often make with websites is that they don't include enough detail.

Sure, most website visitors don't want a jam-packed homepage that scrolls for miles. But you need to make sure that every detail about your hotel is on show, and every potential question is answered on your website – which can be found easily and quickly. Don't put a limit on the amount of pages or information you share online.

Look at your list of objectives for your website. Now look at your website. Are you explaining in enough detail everything a prospective guest will need to know for every item on the list?

Most likely not – or at least, not in enough detail.

You may think that no one wants to read all about your quality standards, or why you only offer certain brands of water or toiletries, or where your meat comes from – but some people do.

A good way to explain why detail sells, is to compare your website to a newspaper or magazine. These publications are read by people in different ways, but they are designed in a way that everyone can find out the latest news, in the amount of detail they want to.

The skim readers look at the **headlines**. The same will be true on websites – so make sure there are headlines and obvious copy on your site that covers all your objectives so that the skim readers will see it – think bold, and use 'ads' and buttons.

If a print headline catches a reader's attention, they might read the **first line or paragraph** for more detail – and this is why journalists are taught to include the key facts in their opening sentences. On a website, this means you need a good clear summary after your headline that covers the key information.

If the first paragraph of an article has the reader hooked, they'll probably **read to the end** – this is where all the detail is. So on your website make sure there is 'more' and somewhere for the reader to go to find out all the detail. If they are interested, they will read it – and this is where you can really sell why you're different. You can achieve this with a landing page packed full of information, or a series of articles on different web pages.

And for the really keen reader there is sometimes a reference for **further reading** at the end of a print article or feature where they can buy related books, or lists of other articles they may be interested in. The website equivalent is to link to more of the detail about what you do to keep the reader on your site. Or you might link to some blog articles or recent news you have on your website – just give the reader options and keep them engaged (and on your site).

The bonus is that search engines **love** content, so the more detail you include in your website, the more chance you have of being found on search engines for that detail.

Action 3.3 Check your content

Go back to your website and see if, for each of the key objectives and benefits of your hotel that you want to communicate, you have:

Headline information

Summary information

More detail

Further reading

You'll probably find you've got some writing to do!

Write down the detail – finding the words

You should now have a list of objectives for your hotel website, and against that list all the gaps where you need to add detail. You're probably also thinking – what do I write? How do I write it?

If you don't see yourself as a 'writer', a good way to write the detail about your hotel is to talk about it into a voice recorder. Either record yourself or ask someone to interview you and record your conversation. You probably know all about why you do things the way you do – why you have the pillows you have, the thinking behind the colour schemes in the rooms, the standards you have for the housekeeping team, and how often you update your menus, but if asked to write this into copy you may suffer from writer's block.

And don't think that people aren't interested in the tiniest detail – some people are.

Make a list of everything you do, how you do it, why you do it, then take a look at it and realise you've got lots of detail. We know hotel owners who clean the taps and chrome in their bathroom with toothbrushes to ensure they are thoroughly clean – that's a great detail to share. And what about all the entertainment and facilities you have. Talk about the detail – don't just say you have 'kids' toys' – explain you've got soft toys and play mats for babies and toddlers, and a Wii for the older kids plus board games, 47 children's DVDs, and giant-sized skittles for outside. Your customers will remember detail. It's what will stick in their minds and helps them remember you and why you are different.

So, if you get stuck with 'writing', just talk it all out and write it up afterwards.

Action 3.4 Add detail to your objectives

Go back to the list you created in Action 3.1 and one by one 'talk' about the detail.

Then think about what in your 'detail' is unique to you. It's all in your head – you just need to get it out.

Write it down.

Tell your readers everything they need to know

Does your website include everything people need to decide they want to stay with you and make a booking? You'd be surprised how many people leave out key information or misprint details.

Go and look at your website **now** to make sure you've got:

Your **location** – full address with postcode, a map (ideally interactive like Google Maps), directions, with local transport links shown.

How to get to you – driving, trains, flying, ferries – cover all modes of transport with walking times, bus and taxi from stations, ports and airports. Indicate prices and provide links to book if you can.

Information about – and photos of – the **surrounding area and local attractions**. Paint the picture of where you are, in relation to other towns, and landmarks.

Prices and packages – include all the options for stays at your hotel – show B&B rates, room only, half board, 24-hour and day delegate rates, dining options that can be decided on the day, package prices and special offers. Your pricing needs to be clear, easy to understand and transparent. If half board represents a £10 saving, then say that – work out all the sums for people, to make their decision-making easier.

Availability – either have an online live calendar of availability or make it easy to check availability with you.

How to contact you – as many ways as possible. Phone, call backs, email, email forms, detailed enquiry forms, online booking, text, Twitter – however you can be reached – include it on your website.

Your rooms – photos of **all** of them if they are different. Room plans or floor plans can also work well to show layouts. Be creative – but also make sure the room is clearly shown. People like to know what they are booking.

Photos of your restaurant, garden, pool, views, lounge, breakfast room, reception, and building – as many photos as you have areas to your hotel.

Sample **menus** if you have a restaurant (or if you only serve breakfast – show it.) Even your **bar list** and **wine list** can be useful to share on your website.

For your **function rooms** give dimensions, layout options, capacity, equipment provided and available for hire, break-out areas, reception space, how much natural light.

Detail your **function catering** options, with sample menus and where refreshments are served.

List (and where possible show photos) of all your **amenities**. If you have a book and DVD library share the list. Have spa menus or local golf course prices available. Anything that your guests have access to – include on your website. It can help with decision-making, and shows your attention to detail.

Action 3.5 Review your key information

Look at the list of key information in this section. Even if you think it's already on your website, have another read through to check that it's:

Up to date

Includes as much detail as you can

Is clear and easy to find and read

Promote your local area

Give your prospects a feel for the area surrounding your hotel and restaurant.

- **Restaurant diners** may wish to combine a visit to other local attractions for a day out.
- **Business users** may want to know what evening entertainment and recreational options are available, such as running routes, pay as you go golf, local cinema or theatre
- **Leisure hotel guests** may want to know bit of the local history, and what else there is to see in the area. Describe these in your own words to show your personality, or ask your staff to describe one of their favourite haunts. All this helps build rapport with the prospect, and helps to influence their buying decision.

Appeal to your guests' eyes and ears

To make the most from your website, ensure that your hotel and restaurant listings are complete and written with full descriptions, with professional photos and videos.

Photographs

As the cliché says, a picture paints a thousand words, so include pictures. But not catalogue pictures if you can help it – ideally photos of real customers – at events, in meetings, eating your food, and having fun.

For both the key information and 'detail' you have on your website you should use photos as much as possible. But you do **also** have to do the words, and this is something many people forget.

So while it is very important to include clear, well-lit, interesting and eye-catching photos on your website, you can't rely in the photos alone to 'sell' your hotel.

Search engines don't 'see' photos – they see the titles, alt tags and descriptions that go with them.

You can get a lot of results on search engines with people searching for 'images' but if you want to get results on text searches, you need to add words to your photos. And remember that it will be your written descriptions across your website content that will be helping you with search engines the most, so it's not **just** about good photography.

Don't simply 'label' your photos – think about how you can use them to add to visitors' experience of your site **and** help you out with the search engines.

Picture	Don't say	Do say
Hotel room	*Hotel Bedroom 5*	*Hotel Splendid's bedroom 5 has west facing sunset views to the South Downs, Sussex with two comfy armchairs placed to enjoy this view*
Bathroom	*Hotel Bedroom 5 bathroom*	*Hotel Splendid's bathrooms use brand posh toiletries, always include two fluffy bath towels per guest, and have under floor heating*
Amenities	*The Pool*	*The Outdoor Swimming Pool at Hotel Splendid is heated year round to a warm 27° C and has plenty of loungers for relaxing on in summer*

Don't underestimate the difference this makes. We see many websites with some great photos on them – but without even a title or label. You know what the photo is of and what you're trying to show – but your potential guest doesn't.

Action 3.6 Review your photos

Look at your website and make sure there are photos of **everything**

Write detailed descriptions to go with your photos to entice the reader

Add keyword-rich titles, tags and descriptions to all your photos for the search engines

Videos

It's now really easy to add video to your hotel website, and it doesn't have to be expensive. You can use videos to convey what's different about your hotel, and get across the personality of the hotel.

Where you can, include virtual tours and video. People like to know what they're getting. You need to answer all the potential questions a prospective guest or diner has. If they want to know if it's dark or light in the rooms, show them. If they want to see if a room is open-plan, or has cosy corners, show them.

YouTube (www.youtube.com) is now considered the second biggest search engine after Google, and people may find your hotel just from its videos. If you have a YouTube channel that hosts all the videos about your hotel, restaurant and area, you have a high chance of being found this way. Reports increasingly suggest that video and virtual tours improve sales conversion on your website.

It's easy to set up a YouTube channel, and equally easy to embed your videos into your website. YouTube give you a code to insert into your website to display the video. Don't worry if you can't present a 'professional' video (a guide for these is £1,000 a minute of video to produce). Some simple videos taken yourself, or some sit-down interviews with you and your staff will work just fine. It's all about showing your personality and the personality of your hotel – so reflect these in your videos, too. Some simple editing with captions and intro screens will add enough credibility to help you get started. Save the professional videos for later, when you see how they help with results.

If you want to share the quiet, relaxed atmosphere, shoot a video that's quiet and relaxed.

If you want to show you have a bustling bar and restaurant every night of the week, take a video of customers enjoying this atmosphere.

Video can certainly help you achieve some of the objectives of your website, so we challenge you to make some short videos and upload them.

Here are some ideas of what you can film:

- Your **rooms** and **amenities**, with a simple voiceover from the owner or manager explaining the detail
- Your **restaurant** or **breakfast room**, with an interview with the chef behind the scenes in your immaculate **kitchen**, as they explain their menu and approach

- The **outside areas** of your hotel – the approach, the garden, the views
- Your local area and **surroundings**
- **Testimonial** interviews with current guests – this is a **great** video to have on your site. There is no doubting the authenticity of testimonials in a video interview
- An **interview** with you, your hotel manager or

owner, discussing your approach to guests' stays, what you offer, your attention to detail, and why people should come and stay with you.

If you want to place it on a 'news' or blog page, do, but a link from the homepage, or embedded where it's relevant to website content, is even better.

And make sure you tag the video with lots of relevant keywords in YouTube, too, to help you get found on this powerful search engine.

Here are a couple of examples:

> *Bournemouth hotel manager Liz Splendid shares tips for a great seaside family holiday on the South Coast of England*
>
> *Romantic weekend hotel breaks in Leeds have all the ingredients for a special short break*

You get a link back to your hotel's website in the listing and also make sure you mention it in the video.

Action 3.7 Make a video

Give it a go! Produce a video for your website – pick a feature or one holiday you offer and make a video to 'showcase' it.

If you already have a video/videos, add another.

(And don't forget to upload your videos to your YouTube channel that you've set up, with lots of keywords in the description.)

Make your website user-friendly

Good website design means people find the information they want – quickly and easily. Is your site easy to navigate? Can people move easily back to the previous page, or the homepage? Is your site well 'signposted' from every page?

Your homepage

Your homepage will often be the 'first impression' of your hotel. It needs to reflect the personality of your hotel, and be very clear about who it's targeted at. So it's an important page to get right.

You need to make sure there are clear links from here to all the key areas of information about your hotel. You also need to have clear messages and images that prospective guests will quickly identify with you to know 'they are in the right place'. **Every website visitor comes to your site with a question – make sure they can answer it**.

Ensure there are links from your homepage – ideally eye-catching visual ones – that take prospective guests straight to the key information and the answers to their questions:

- Where are you?
- How much are your rooms/packages?
- What are your rooms like?
- What amenities are there?
- Any special offers?

- How do I contact you or book?
- What's your availability?
- What food do you serve in your restaurant?
- What makes you different – why should I book with you?

By a visual link we mean a button or header that clearly signposts where the reader can find information if they click on it.

Think of your homepage as a place to advertise your hotel and services and show prospective guests exactly what you do and where to find out more information about it.

If you are ideal for couples, families and friends – say so clearly in your homepage.

If your hotel is the perfect venue for business team building events – say so, and why this is so.

If you pride yourself on having the best breakfast or beds or swimming pool or whatever amenities you have that make you **stand out** – your homepage is the place to **shout about them**.

Action 3.8 Review your homepage

Take a good look at your homepage

Does it meet the objectives you set out in Action 3.1?

Use the checklist here to see if all questions are answered

What changes do you need to make? **Now make them!**

Keep your design simple

You don't have to have the fanciest design in the world – although having clear, well thought out, proven layout will help enormously. Choose colours and fonts that work well for your target market and tie in with your brand.

Your website should be easy to read and attractive to look at. Don't have any key information or actions you want visitors to take 'below the fold' on the homepage, i.e. where people have to scroll, as you can't guarantee they'll see it.

Have contact information very clear and visible on your website pages (the top right in the header is a typical and expected place to find this on a website).

On every page of your website, but particularly the homepage, you need compelling 'next actions' to encourage the reader to find out more. Do this with words **and** pictures. We discuss having a clear call to action on page 99.

Downloads

Make it easy for people to print out or download information about your hotel and services. Not everyone will decide to book while looking at the screen. They may want to print out information to show others, or forward to others.

So create PDFs of key information or make mini brochures available. Have a 'print this page' option on your website, too.

Ask for feedback

Now you've taken a look at your homepage, and added in key navigation and calls to action, you should get other people to look at your website. A good way to get feedback is to ask people some questions to see how easy and obvious your site layout really is for them to find the answers.

For example, you could ask people to look up:

- How much is a one-night stay in April?
- What options are there for eating at or near the hotel?
- Pick out the room you'd want to have for a special occasion

- How can you get to the hotel from London? (Or if already in London – from somewhere else).
- What is the availability for 2–6 November (and if you can't see this, how easy is it to find out where to ask for availability)
- Why is your hotel better than others in your location?
- What capacity do you have for functions and seminars?

Setting people questions to answer can be better than just asking for their feedback. But still give your testers the chance to comment on their overall impression and experience of using your site, as you'll often get unexpected, useful feedback. Ask them: What did you most like about the website? What did you not like?

Don't forget to ask people to review your website who are in line with your ideal customers and target audience to make sure the feedback you get is relevant. There's no point asking great Aunt Mabel to take a look if you cater for 20-something couples who are online-savvy, or to ask the 15-year-old next door to look if your site is aimed at 30–40 something mums taking their young families on holiday.

Action 3.9 Get feedback on your website

> Ask 5–10 target market prospects to take a look at your new homepage and website. Set them questions to find the answers to
>
> Also don't forget to ask guests for their feedback on the website. Could they find all the information they were looking for? Did they book online?

Review your booking system

How do people book from your website? Make it easy, make it obvious, and offer multiple options to get in touch. Different people prefer different methods of contact or booking, so offer everything you can.

If you're happy to, give the option to book rooms online, or simply to check availability and prices for the dates in question. This can save you and your staff a lot of time.

However, many guests (and hotel owners) prefer email or phone to make a booking, so make sure this is an easy option. A 0800 number can encourage people to call you, while an expensive premium number can put people off.

If your reception or switchboard is not manned 24 hours a day, say when it **is** manned (and show the times clearly on your website). Many of your potential guests will be searching during the evening or at weekends. So consider offering a call back service, or pay for an out-of-hours answering service. If a prospective guest can't talk to you, they may well find another hotel they can talk to.

Give the option of an online enquiry, as well as an option to open up a blank email. Having a simple 'ask us a question' form can be helpful as it's more inviting (and less committed) than a 'make an enquiry' or 'make a booking' form.

Don't forget other options – post, social media sites (e.g. Twitter or Facebook, see page 158), texting, or a mobile app or optimised website. Align your booking system with your ideal guests.

You don't want to miss an enquiry or booking just because you don't offer a contact option the way someone wants to contact you.

Action 3.10 Review your booking system

How do people book with you:

Online? – review your booking forms, enquiries, ask a question, email address?

By phone? – is 24 hour coverage taken care of? Does your website show your 'office hours'

By email? – who picks up these emails? How quickly are they answered?

Can they check **availability status** live on your website?

From overseas? – offer alternative phone numbers and the international dialling code

Another way? How do your ideal customers want to book? Text message? Twitter?

Check your links

Make sure all the links on your website work, especially your booking forms and emails. Keep your content and links across the site up to date and correct – you don't want to lose anyone at the last hurdle when they're ready to book and your website lets you down.

Few prospective customers will bother to let you know if there's a problem with your website; they will just give up and find somewhere else and book there instead.

So spend some time today checking through and testing your website.

And schedule this as a regular check to carry out. It might sound simple, but you'd be surprised how broken links and email forms that don't work can go unnoticed.

If you update your site a lot it can be easy to make mistakes, or miss an edit that can change a functioning link to a broken one.

Test the browsers

You also need to make sure your website looks the same and works on all the main web browsers. A good web designer will always test a new website on the latest main web browsers and make sure the site works on all of them, including PCs and Macs. You need to make sure most people looking at your site will see it how you want them to.

In Lucy's website design business, for example, all new websites are currently tested on Internet Explorer, Firefox and Safari – on both a PC and a Mac. It's worth loading up more than one browser on your machine to do these checks on a regular basis.

Have more than one website

You don't have to limit yourself to one website. You must have a main website – it's rare these days to find a booker or guest who won't at least give a cursory glance at your website (and more often than not they'll have a good look around it!), but you can have other websites, too.

Landing pages

If you're offering specific holiday packages, a special offer or a niche service, think about having a 'landing page' website – a destination page that **only** sells a particular campaign or offer.

With a landing page, you can attract and direct traffic to just **one** offer or holiday that you want to promote and only include information relevant to that offer. It can work really well. There is only one call to action on a landing page (**book now** or **enquire now**) and you want a 'yes/no' response.

An example landing page could be for a one-off event or offer such as a ballroom dancing evening with DB&B, tennis coaching weekend with B&B, fancy dress lunch – any one event or offer you can build a landing page for.

Microsites

Or you could have a number of **microsites** (small websites with just a few pages) for each different target market or specific services or packages you offer.

Each site would have a different web address and show in detail why you're the best at providing this one holiday or service, but would leave out the detail of everything else you offer – because it isn't relevant to this customer.

Landing pages and microsites are not as costly as you might think – if you ask a web designer to build you a template, each page or site can follow the same format but have its own specific content.

If you have more websites, you can produce stand-alone flyers and brochures and point them to websites that appeal to different customers or promote different holidays and offers. The same is true for any online advertising. Because the sites are only about **one** offer or holiday, you can easily track and measure which campaigns and offers are working for you.

You can take one of your markets and tailor a microsite just for them – families, spa lovers, foodies, or business people. Or you can tailor a microsite for a season – Christmas holidays, half-term breaks, or a type of stay – golfing holidays, learn a language weekends. The microsite will only contain information relevant to the topic in each case, so it's very focused on its job of selling **only** this holiday type or to this market.

Maximise your online visibility

If you want people to look at your website – make sure they can see it!

First, research the keywords that your perfect customers type into their search engine to find you. Google has a free keyword tool (www.adwords.google.com) to help you out. Don't guess the keywords and phrases perfect customers might use – **find out**!

You might think your guests search on '4 star hotel Bath' but they might actually be searching for 'luxury holiday Bath city'. You need to know what words they're using. Then you need to 'talk' your guests' language.

Make sure your website copy includes the keywords guests use when searching on the web. Use headings that include your keywords and page titles, too. This is all SEO (Search Engine Optimisation). There are many other things you can do to help with SEO, and it's worth consulting some experts, but keywords are the minimum you should think about.

Don't 'fight' for the obvious keywords either – people search for all sorts of things. The 'longtail' (a longer, more specific search phrase) is often the key to getting really good, qualified traffic to your website.

Here's an example: if you and 50 other hotels are fighting over 'Newquay Hotel', look up all the keywords and phrases about your ideal customers and what you do. You might be better off with these five phrases than fighting over 'Newquay Hotel':

- family holidays with toddlers in Newquay
- luxury family hotel near beach in Newquay

- surf beach holiday Cornwall luxury hotel couples
- Cornwall beach holiday with children hotel near sea family suites
- holidays in Newquay babysitting available

This is especially important when you start to look at paid online advertising – as if you're fighting over the same 'headline' keywords and phrases as everyone else, expect to spend a lot of money!

But while we are talking about natural search (search engine results based on the content of your website, that you're not paying for) the same principle applies, but this time the 'cost' is between being seen and not being seen on Google (or another search engine).

Because you've already identified who your perfect customers are and what they're looking for, it's going to be **much** better for you to come up on the top of page 1 of Google for 'family holidays with toddlers in Newquay' than to be lower down page 1 or on 2, 3 or 4 for 'Newquay Hotel'.

You may get a 1-in-10 conversion rate for your holidays if you already attract your perfect customer with 'what they're looking for' on your website than if you just go for more general appeal. People typing 'Newquay Hotel' could be looking for anything from a cheap B&B to a luxury hotel, and they could have any number of preferences, budgets and requirements. You might be lucky to convert 1/100 or 1/1000 of these.

Having a clear picture of your ideal customer will impact on **all** your marketing and make it more successful. Marketing is not a 'numbers game' – it's about the **quality** of your leads, not the **quantity**.

It's better to reach 100 prospects who are all 100% your ideal customers than 1000 prospects who could be anyone. Your mantra for online marketing should be: Target, target, target – niche, niche, niche!

Your perfect customers are out there and you need to concentrate all your efforts as far as you can on **only** targeting them, and not worrying about 'everyone'.

Natural search listings are very important. Unless you're listed on the first page or so of a search engine, it's unlikely that people will find your website this way. Don't get hung up on 'vanity phrases' (that you think you should be listed under (e.g. Luxury hotel Newquay) or fight over the obvious key phrases, as this can be a wasted effort. Look closely at what **your** perfect customers are searching for by asking your existing customers and measuring the current keywords that are converting to sales in your website traffic). Make sure your website is found for the phrases your ideal customers **do** search for (even if they're longer and more specific.).

Action 3.11 Brainstorm key words and phrases

Brainstorm key words and phrases related to your hotel, the holidays, facilities and services you offer.

Look up the popularity of these phrases using a keyword tool.

Decide on which phrases you want to compete (remember less popular phrases are still searched for - more focus and less competition is good).

Keep your website up-to-date

Promotions that are out-of-date or events that have already passed are not only unhelpful but make it look as if you don't care (even if you do).

A regularly updated site will improve your search rankings better than one that is left unchanged. Search engines rate sites on content and relevancy, so are looking for new content each time they come to your site. Make sure you're giving search engines new content all the time to push you up the rankings and likelihood of being found.

Ensure that you (or someone in your team) can update your website content in-house, or easily. For a reminder of why it's a really good idea to have a content management system for your website, see page 57.

You must be able to respond to your market with new events, last-minute promotions, current availability, tariff changes, travel bulletins, seasonal messages, and so on. You then know you can be quick to offer tailored packages and holidays that you can link to from campaigns.

Update daily

If you think of a new offer first thing in the morning you should be able to get it live on your website, your blog and your social networking sites that same morning. If you can't respond to events and news like this, it could mean missing out to a competitor who can.

Tailor your site for visitors from abroad

If you want to attract visitors from abroad, you'll need to tailor your site, as this will be the key way people will find out about your hotel. Even if you use travel agents overseas, it's very likely prospective guests will also 'Google' you.

This doesn't mean having a website in 47 languages. Identify which nationalities you want to attract. What overseas visitors does your area attract? (Ask your tourist office for statistics.) Think about transport links, including cheap ferries or budget airline routes, and for business trade review your local businesses and the countries they trade with.

Translating your whole site might be costly. We suggest that you have some landing pages that provide the key information about your hotel, links to images, and your booking forms in other languages if that's part of your target market. Convert your prices to Euros if you're aiming for the European market, for example.

Your keywords and content may not translate directly into the language, so you may need to look at these and change these to suit the search terms that natives of your target market would use.

We've all had a giggle on holiday over poor translations into English on menus and signs. Avoid this problem by using a professional translator. You can find one through the Institute of Translating and Interpreting, www.iti.org.uk.

We don't recommend that you use an online tool to translate your web pages. You wouldn't know if there were mistakes and the information could be misleading. This is especially key for your bookings page, where the correct information is essential. Check with your booking provider as they may already offer European languages as standard, or ensure any instructions you have for emails are in other languages, too.

Microsites (small websites) for different overseas markets are also a good option for having all the information that is important to this market about your hotel and area. See more about microsites on page 83.

If you advertise to overseas guests in their language but don't have staff at the hotel who speak these languages, make that clear on your website and printed material, too. You want guests to feel welcome and able to communicate, so be clear about what you can and can't offer. And if you know you can access tour guides, drivers or any facilities in your area where overseas languages are catered for, promote these too.

Chapter 3 recap

In this chapter, we've covered:

- ✓ Managing your website so that you can keep it up to date and focused
- ✓ Measuring your website traffic and performance with analytics
- ✓ Checking that you've included everything your guests and prospects need to know on your website – and that it's clear where to find it
- ✓ Having a clear design that makes booking with you easy
- ✓ Making good use of photos and videos
- ✓ Having more than one website – such as a landing page or microsite for niche marketing, offers and specific services
- ✓ Maximising your online visibility by improving your natural search engine results

Authors' comments

Caroline: I am certainly not a 'techie', and most hotel owners and managers I work with aren't either, so the idea of editing a website can be pretty daunting (I know it was for me.). But having a simple to use and intuitive content management system makes anyone a web designer (well, editor at least!). I know when I switched my own business site to WordPress it meant I could update and add to the site where and when I wanted to.

Lucy: I am very aware that I help design, build and run websites for a living and so what to me is everyday language and know-how, to the majority of business owners it's still somewhat of a mystery! But you're not alone – and always ask questions if you don't understand anything that your web designer says to you. A good website company should be able to tell you exactly what they're doing with your site, why, and how that's going to help your hotel. Well, that's what we do anyway! And don't forget – get a website that **you** can edit, and is hosted independently so you'll always have control over this very valuable asset.

Chapter 4

Communication

Chapter 4

Communication

Now you have a clear picture of your identity, guests and offering, it's time to bring these elements together and think about the way you communicate with your customers, both online and offline.

When we say 'communication' we mean the messages, tone and language that you will use to reach your guests and potential guests in your marketing and sales efforts. Communication incorporates written and spoken words, and the impression that you convey to guests in all your materials and contact with them.

In this chapter, we explain how to:

- ✓ Write advertising copy that puts you in your guests' shoes and answers the question 'What's in it for me?
- ✓ Use a sales formula to attract, interest, arouse desire and call your customers to action
- ✓ Choose and use the best communication channels for your hotel
- ✓ Show yourself in your best light
- ✓ Prompt bookings by creating a sense of scarcity or urgency
- ✓ Give different options for responding to your offers

- ✓ Build and manage your mailing list
- ✓ Grow your mailing list using offers and incentives
- ✓ Keep in touch with your guests and prospects

Write compelling advertising copy

Good advertising copy is not all about you. It's always about your customer and what you can do for them.

When you read it back, put yourself in their shoes and ask yourself 'What's in it for me to come and stay at this hotel?' If you can't answer that question, look at your copy again. People aren't interested in how long you've been in business or where you trained or how old the building is (unless you make it about them if they're history buffs!). What they're interested in is what these things add to their experience.

Long copy normally outsells short copy, so **go into detail.** The same rules apply for online and offline. If you struggle with your copy, outsource it to a copywriter, but check they have experience of copywriting in a marketing context. You might be the best person to 'talk' about what you do, so record your words, but get help 'writing' them if you need it.

Advertising copy is the conversation you have with your potential and existing guests about what they'll experience when they stay with you. It needs to flow, be packed with your personality and not stilted or too formal. If your content is going on the web, you also need to pack it with keywords that your customers use and relate to. (See page 84).

Action 4.1 Put yourself in your guests' shoes

Put yourself (or a friend or colleague) in your guests' shoes and ask yourself:
What's in it for me to stay in this hotel?

(Your answers from Chapter 1– Identity and emotional/physical/results description might be helpful.)

Use a sales formula

The most commonly recognised and powerful copywriting formula is AIDA:

- **A**ttention
- **I**nterest
- **D**esire
- **A**ction

Any promotional copy must begin with the statement that grabs your readers' **attention**. How will your offer help your customer, or what needs does it satisfy? This could be an obvious statement, a question, something topical, any headline to attract attention.

Here are some examples of grabbing attention with a headline:

- *Why the best 5 star hotels copy what we do – when hotel stars don't guarantee a star studded experience*
- *How to de-stress in 24 hours – 1 night in a hotel can change your life*

- *The 9 essential ingredients for a truly memorable honeymoon*
- *Solve your family holiday dilemma in 5 minutes*
- *Why the Isle of Wight is the new Jamaica*

Headline writing is an art in itself – and without a good headline it almost doesn't matter how good the rest of your copy is, as no one will get that far! This is when it makes sense to test different headlines, reflect on the key phrases that work for you online, ask your customers what they respond to, and get help with your copywriting if you need it.

Once you've passed the headline hurdle, keep your customers' **interest** by providing more information – what makes it different. Give as much detail as you need to illustrate your point.

Arouse your customers' **desire**; describe what you provide in a way that is irresistible.

And always give your customers a **call to action** – a reason to respond now, before they turn the page, put the insert down, or click away.

Here's a full example:

> **Attention:** *Solve your family holiday dilemma in 5 minutes*
>
> **Interest:** *With awards for our crèche facilities, teen club converts who beg their parents to return to stay with us every year, a state of the art spa and onsite tennis and golf, we've had families stay with us summer after summer who used to holiday in the Med religiously.*
>
> **Desire:** *The envy of their friends, the families that manage to secure a booking with us are in for a treat. Nothing is more relaxing than a holiday that has something for everyone, so every member of the family is happy – all holiday. If all you can think about is indulging yourself – either relaxing or enjoying your favourite pastime all day without worrying about your kids (who will be having a much better time with out you if you want them to!) then you know where to book your next holiday.*
>
> **Action:** *To make sure you have the family holiday you deserve book now – call xxxxxx or complete this form. Upgraded suites are allocated on a first come first served basis so don't delay.*

 Action 4.2 Put AIDA into practice

Think how you are going to:

Attract your potential customers with a headline statement

Interest your customers with information that is different about your hotel

Arouse your customers' **desire** by making your offer irresistible

Give a call to **action** – a reason to respond straight away

Use the right communication channels

Knowing and understanding your guests is critical when thinking about the media you'll use to promote your business.

In Chapter 1 you identified your guests' needs and expectations. This will help determine the types of message that will appeal to your customer, the most appropriate style of communication and the language they use.

You need to know this about your customers:

- What **types of message** will appeal to them? e.g. something that offers value for money or something exclusive and unique that they couldn't get anywhere else.

- What **style** of communication would be most relevant to them? e.g. fun and funky or family focused, 'sexy' and indulgent or no-nonsense and business-like.
- What type of **language** do they use? e.g. how your wording may be different if written to attract young beach lovers compared with mature couples.

Now we need to consider the most appropriate channels:

- What publications do they read, where do they socialise?
- Where do they spend their time?
- What access do they have to the Internet?

All of these factors influence the ways in which you attract more business and retain existing customers. So think back to the profile of your ideal customer from Action 1.1 before working out **where** to find them, and **how** to communicate with them.

And don't forget – if you **really** want to understand your guests' preference for communication – you **must ask them.**

No one can tell you which campaigns and messages will work best for you until you try them on **your** customers and **measure the results**.

You'll never be able to 100% gauge the reaction and response to your customers. This is where testing and analysis (see page 60) are vital in any of your marketing campaigns. Think about the people you're communicating with and tailor your campaign to them.

Action 4.3 Identify your communication channels

Ask yourself:

How I am going to communicate with my customers?

What types of message will appeal to them?

What style of communication would be most relevant to them?

What type of language do they use?

What publications do they read?

Where do they socialise?

Where do they spend their time?

What access do they have to the Internet?

Show yourself in your best light

Ensure all your promotional material conveys the right message and is consistent with the product or service, as well as your brand image and values. Much of what you are selling is based on the senses and emotion (see page 24), so use these in your promotional material. You and your team also have to 'be' these values, too.

For example, if you are promoting an exclusive and luxurious room and services at your hotel, the wording, the style and quality of the promotional material should look exclusive and feel luxurious. If you're promoting a thirst-quenching drink, which is served ice-cold, your promotional material needs to conjure up this image, through the images, colour, and wording, and maybe even the positioning of the material (in an ice bucket, not next to the log fire). If promoting a family fun-filled holiday, your material, colours, images and wording should be vibrant and lively too.

Action 4.4 Think about the look and feel of your promotional material

What images do you want to show?

What colours do you want to use?

What words are going to attract your ideal guest? (Make sure it's language **they** use)

Create scarcity and urgency

You can prompt an immediate booking by creating a sense of scarcity or urgency in your messages.

For example, to create **scarcity** (not many), limit an offer to the first 10 customers who book; state the maximum number of people you can accommodate for a particular event; let people know when you only have three rooms left for a popular date.

To create a sense of **urgency** (not long), impose a deadline on your offer or a deadline for booking. The shorter the time frames, the better to prompt action. But do ensure that you're confident about the timing; you'll shoot yourself in the foot if your offer goes out after the deadline has passed.

So make sure all offers that have expired are no longer available on your website or to book. However, you can show the offer on your website but as 'no longer available' or 'fully booked'. This reminds people to be quick next time an offer like this comes along! That way the offer carries on working even after it's expired.

Action 4.5 Make offers scarce or urgent

How can you make your offer(s) 'scarce'? For example, 'first 10' 'only 3 rooms available'.

Can you put a deadline on your offer(s) to make it 'urgent'?

What will you do when you are fully booked or the deadline is reached? (Have a plan)

Give options for responding to your offers

Different people will prefer different ways of getting in touch.

Not everyone has access to the Internet all the

time; so always include a contact phone number (including the best times to call if this line is not manned 24/7). If you do have literature to send by post, (a comparatively expensive option these days) you could use inserts or flyers as a prepaid card to post back to you.

With any print advertising, include your offline and online contact details, and always include a code so that you can track the source of the enquiry and measure the performance of different adverts.

You may want to offer a dedicated email address for an offer (which is easy to set up) or collect enquiries from a landing page either on your website or stand alone (either way with a URL unique to that ad or offer to track results) (see page 83 for more about landing pages).

Whatever your chosen contact options, make sure you test they work, and that everyone who will deal with the enquiries – online, on the phone, by post – knows all the details of the offers.

Action 4.6 Identify your contact options

Write down all your contact options, with special numbers, addresses or promotional codes, and opening times:

Telephone number

What will you say on your voice-mail message?

Fax number

Email

Online form

In person

Build a mailing list

Your customer mailing list is one of the most valuable assets of your hotel.

When we started in business and people referred to their 'list' we completely underestimated the importance of this. Building a list of existing customers and prospects is critical to building your business.

Without a list, every time you want to get something in front of your guests or prospects you have to start all over again. Your list gives you the opportunity to tell every existing and potential customer about promotions, seasonal events and any other newsworthy information relevant to your niche.

What information you capture on your list will depend on how you're going to use it. The essentials are a guest or prospect's name and some form of contact address, either postal or email or both. You may want to get phone numbers, too. And in an ideal world you compile a profile of interests, likes and dislikes and anything else that will help you communicate with that contact that's personal to them.

Additional information to consider would be anything that would help you segment your prospects, and anything that will help you to target prospects and customers for particular offers or timing of offers. Examples would be:

- birthdays and anniversaries
- dates of booking
- dates of visit
- interests or hobbies
- source of initial contact (via website, advert local paper, travel agent)
- age or demographic
- what newspaper and/or magazines they read.

The more detail you have on people who are interested in what you offer, the more often you can return to them with additional offers that are tailored to them. And the more often you do this, the more likely it is that this will result in business.

Asking for a lot of personal detail up front is, however, not very practical (and likely to be very off putting) so it's better to gather it over time.

Action 4.7 Information about your prospects and customers

Think about the information you want to hold about your prospects and customers that sets them out as ideal customers.

Which is the most important, and which can wait until you know them better?

Manage your contacts

Invest in a list management system to safeguard your valuable contacts. To manage your list, you'll need a system to capture the details, keep them all in order, and help you manage your communications to them.

You could do this using:

- a simple email or list management system; or
- a full-blown CRM (Customer Relationship Management) system

The choice is yours. Whichever you use, ensure you have a backup – having worked so hard to get people's details you won't want to lose them.

Many booking systems include contact management systems, so make the most of this facility if you have it, or invest in a stand-alone CRM system. CRM does not need to be expensive and there are many online options that cost just a few pounds a month.

If all you need is an email list management system, again look for an online solution and you will find low cost and even free options.

Email management

If you intend to contact people on your list by email, the easiest way to set this up is with an email management system.

The advantages of these are that:

- They'll automate much of the procedure of building and keeping a database.
- They store all of your subscriptions or enquiries.
- You can send an automated email response or series of emails by return when enquiries are made online.
- You can segment your list into different categories, or manage different lists, so you can send relevant messages only to those to whom they apply.
- You can personalise messages you send out in the same way as creating a mail merge (with a first name greeting, for example).
- They can be relatively inexpensive.

Many email systems are web-based – all your information is stored on the Internet rather than on your computer, so if your computer crashes you know that your list is still secure.

Aweber (www.aweber.com) is an example of an email management system that is simple to set up and use. MailChimp (www.mailchimp.com) is another email system that provides an easy way to manage your list, and it also offers a free service.

Customer relationship manager (CRM)

If you are thinking about using a CRM, research your requirements carefully and then opt for a system that will integrate with your existing business processes and add value.

If you only need email management, a CRM may be an unnecessary expense. But if you want to monitor and capture more information about your prospects and customers, CRM is the answer. You can opt for an online solution or one that's installed on your computer. Online systems are typically 'pay as you go' monthly, and allow you and your colleagues access to them from anywhere with an Internet connection.

Examples of online CRM systems are Highrise, Salesforce and Capsule.

You can also have an installed CRM system (where you will load the software and hold all your own data on your own computers) such as Microsoft CRM, ACT, and Goldmine.

Action 4.8 Review your contact management

Look at your current business processes and systems to see if you need to set up an email management system or a CRM.

If you already have a CRM, run a review to see if you are using it to its best efforts.

If you don't already have a list, or way of easily managing or segmenting your contacts set this up now.

When evaluating a new solution, look for compatibility with other existing systems. It usually makes sense to go with a system that already has integration with other software you use (e.g. your booking system, your accounts system, your database)

Offer incentives to build your list

To build your list, you may need to set up incentives for people to fill in a physical form or coupon, or sign up online and share their details. If you're doing this online, this may be in the form of discounts or free downloads such as a guide to something of relevant interest to your target market.

Here are a few ideas to encourage your list to grow:

- A **gift voucher** to spend with you or one of your joint venture partners - see page 232 - this could be services or maybe branded products. A win–win–win for you, your joint venture partner and the customer.
- For your **restaurant** – Voucher for two for one on main meals, free starters or dessert, kids under 7 eat free, all of which encourage customers to the restaurant.
- For **leisure hotels** – any of the above, or local free maps, books on the local area, free entry to attractions, a personally written guide by you, recipes from your chef, etc.
- For **conference or corporate venues** –

invitation to lunch, bring a guest and just pay for your own meal, 50% discount on meeting room hire, book your visitors in and receive one night's complimentary B&B for the organiser here or at a joint venture hotel.

- Where you can, aim to offer **unique** offers, guides, information, and incentives so they aren't a 'standard' that others can copy. You can write your own guides, for example.

To capture people's details online, you need a 'landing page' or sign-up form on your website where people supply their details (see page 83). Your aim is to capture the details of as many potential guests as you can, so you need a really enticing offer to attract even those who may not want to buy right now. They may have either just stumbled on your website, or have seen your advertisement or article elsewhere, and have specifically gone to your landing page to take you up on your offer.

If all you need at first is their name and email address, just ask for that. It's a widely accepted online marketing rule that the more information you ask for, the lower the number of sign-ups you'll have. There may be exceptions, and of course you can test this in your own market.

Gathering details offline, you're more likely to capture the details of existing customers. Ask them to register by completing a form you give them with their bill so they receive exclusive offers, to be kept up-to-date with promotions and special events. For corporate users, this might be as simple as leaving their business card.

Ask your joint venture partners to give their customers your discount vouchers or an invitation to receive your exclusive offers. Then ask customers to complete their details in order to redeem them with you.

You can use contact information taken from guests' registration details, but use this sparingly and only for a follow up and very relevant offers. You're legally entitled to contact your own customers with future offers, but ideally always **seek permission** to use guests' details for any marketing activity. And of course if any guest asks not to be contacted at any time, you must respect this, and record their preference on your database.

Whichever way you capture prospects' and customers' contact information, under the Data Protection Act 1998 you **must** have permission to communicate with them. The Information Commissioner's Office website (www.ico.gov.uk) shows what you need to do.

Action 4.9 Building your list

Identify what incentives you can offer in exchange for people's contact details

How will you capture details?

Run competitions and prize draws

Competitions can encourage people to respond to an offer or join your mailing list, if the prizes are appropriate. Make the competition relevant to your business and appealing to your target market.

You can offer prizes from your own products or services or do a joint venture with another business (offering their products and services). Your first objective is to get entrants' details by offering something they're compelled to respond to, so whatever it is, just ensure it will be irresistible to your target audience.

Unless you do a monthly draw, competitions will have a finite life, so once the closing date for the draw has passed you'll need to introduce some other incentive to capture details. This encourages you to vary your offer, and keep it fresh.

Even if someone didn't respond to your first offer, don't exclude them from future offers.

Action 4.10 Competition ideas

What do you (or could you) offer that would make an irresistible prize?

Thinking about your ideal customers, what other prizes or incentives would appeal (this will help you to think about suitable joint venture partners who can offer these prizes if you cannot)

Increase the frequency of contact

Out of sight is out of mind – so don't disappear from view. Once you have your list, use it to communicate to prospects and customers regularly. Just because somebody hasn't booked with you initially doesn't mean to say that they won't do so in the future (or make a recommendation).

Many marketers say that prospective customers need seven 'touches' before they'll buy a product or service. So the more you communicate and build up trust and rapport, the easier it will be for them to decide to book with you. You're aiming to create a **strong emotional bond** with prospects and customers over time. But don't interpret this advice to mean you can 'spam' prospects with a ton of offers and deals that bombards them and makes them hit the unsubscribe button. They may also tell their friends to avoid you.

One of the simplest things to do is to write a **thank-you note** (not just a customer satisfaction survey) to all guests who have stayed or eaten with you within a few days of their visit. This is a great way to build rapport, and even if they didn't pick up a business card or a brochure when they visited, they'll now have something by which to remember you.

Don't stop at emails – this is the least you can do. If you have postal addresses for guests you can send **letters and postcards**. Different formats of communication, remember, will appeal to different customers, so use a variety of methods. Make people want to open and read your mail by writing compelling subject lines and eye-catching envelopes. A handwritten envelope will always grab attention. And when sending emails, make it clear who the email has come from to avoid suspicion and landing straight in the spam folder. Use the telephone or text, as a follow up to other media; these are a great way to promote last-minute offers or to remind people when an offer is about to expire.

Face-to-face meetings – with an appointment – are worth trying if you can afford it. This may be the best way to build a relationship with businesses in the area, and show the level of service you offer.

What to talk about

What you write or talk about will depend on your target market and their interests.

You may want to adopt a different theme each time to maintain that level of interest, or maybe you could send out a series of articles.

Let your readers know what other people think of you; when you've been featured in the press, for example, or any awards you've been given, or maybe a testimonial from a VIP.

You might also write about recommended places to go or things to do while in the area, maybe with your own account of visits to these places with photographs. Maybe ask your head chef to write something about dishes on the menu with a recipe. Perhaps one of your customers might have interesting experiences of their visit to you to share with others. All of these things add up to paint a picture and give your hotel personality, making the choice that bit easier for your customers and prospects.

Keeping in contact with your list is not about sending them offer after offer but just a way of 'keeping them up to date' with what you're doing. You'll sometimes have an offer for them, but this isn't the sole purpose of every communication. Be creative, be personality-led, but above all, make it interesting and relevant to your customers.

Action 4.11 Contacting your list

What methods could you use to contact your list?
What contact details do you already have?
What else is needed?
How will you gather contact information?
What topics could you write about within the next month?

Make targeted offers to your list

Tell the people on your list whenever you're running a promotion. Segment your list so that you personalise anything you send to that target audience. Then design your promotions to target different customer profiles from your list.

Don't just tell them about it once, either. Build up a bit of suspense – a sort of drum roll to the launch of a promotion or new menu. Once it's launched, send more details, giving updates of how it's going. Let them know what they're missing, and finally give them that last chance to book with a reminder when the promotion or offer is coming to an end.

Use your list to check for birthdays and anniversaries. Send an invitation or an exclusive offer or gift to redeem at the restaurant or hotel. Keep the time frames limited to add a sense of urgency.

Send your business users lunch menus, and note their important dates to offer special deals for seminars, meetings and awards dinners.

If all you ever do is send out offers and deals, and nothing of interest to your readers, they'll quickly unsubscribe from your list.

That said, you can always ask contacts on your list if they want to be on an 'offers only' list and use it accordingly. It's all about managing your 'conversation' with your list – if they want deals send them deals, if they just want news, ideas, tips, and updates, send them those.

Action 4.12 Targeted offers

What events or promotions have you planned that you need to announce to your list?

What messages do you need to convey?

Plan your sequence of mailings for the next month/3 months/+ so you have a plan of regular contact.

Chapter 4 recap

In this chapter, we've shown you how to:

- ✓ Write **advertising copy** that puts you in your customers' shoes and answers the question 'What's in it for me?'
- ✓ Use a sales formula (AIDA) to **attract**, **interest,** arouse **desire** and call your customers to **action** when you communicate
- ✓ Choose and use the best **communication channels** for your sales and marketing messages
- ✓ Show yourself in your **best light** by writing something interesting about what you do, and why it's different
- ✓ Prompt bookings by creating a sense of **scarcity** or **urgency**
- ✓ Give **different options** for responding to your offers

- ✓ Build and manage your **mailing list**
- ✓ **Grow your mailing list** using offers and incentives
- ✓ **Keep in touch** with your customers and prospects – the importance of being targeted in your conversations.

Authors' comments

Caroline: Don't worry if you don't get everything right first time – some of the people I work with take a while to get into the swing of things – but the more you do, the easier it gets. I suggest you always keep a notepad handy to jot down ideas of topics to share with your guests.

Lucy: Be observant – look at and listen to what other hotels and in fact any other businesses are doing to promote themselves. Sometimes inspiration can come from the unlikeliest places! If you are using the same language as your guests you're halfway there – the next is to **test, test, test** until you hit on the triggers that make them book. I don't ever pretend to have 'all the answers' when I work with business owners on their marketing, as it's always about finding out exactly what works for their business and customers. What I do is make a plan, give direction and stress (over and over) the importance of constant monitoring, reflection and adjustment to keep improving results.

Chapter 5

Add value to increase spend and frequency

Chapter 5

Add value to increase spend and frequency

Anything that adds value will attract attention and stimulate sales, providing that people know about it.

To give people an incentive to try you out or make a return visit, and set you apart from the competition, ensure you offer value for money. Value for money does **not** mean low prices necessarily, so here are some ideas of how to avoid that with smart sales and marketing ideas.

This chapter will enable you to:

- ✓ Ensure your **pricing** reflects value for money to your perfect guest
- ✓ Identify how to encourage existing and prospective guests to **try something new**
- ✓ Identify scores of **offers, deals and promotion ideas** to add value without having to offer discounts
- ✓ Plan what you can offer to attract the attention of those who share an interest in your **'expert' topic**
- ✓ **Team up with others** to help you offer value for money
- ✓ **Reverse the risk** to your ideal guest in choosing your hotel

How do you increase your guests' perception of value for money?

A lot will depend on your target audience, and what they place a high value on. The trick for you is to identify what is of **high value** to your guest (and even if they are not prepared to pay a premium price for it, is it still something that will grab their attention?), and is of relatively **low cost** to you. Offering value for money is **not** about compromising on your margins – quite the opposite. It should help you to achieve them.

Get your basic offer right

No amount of offers, deals or specials will ever persuade your guests that you offer value for money if you don't have the basics right.

So ensure you offer a quality product with first-class guest service – consistently. It's not enough to just meet guests' expectations – you need to exceed them. This starts at the point they make their booking and continues as they drive into the car park or walk in through the front door.

Don't just compete on price

Think back to Chapter 1 and your perfect guest. What do they perceive as good value? How do you translate this into your pricing? It's not what **you** see as value or what you would be prepared to pay or be able to pay – it's what **your guests** are wiling or able to pay.

How do you compare with your direct competition? You need to know with **whom** you are likely to be compared, and then **how** you compare with them. Why compare yourself to the unrated budget hotel down the road aiming for backpackers if your target market is business guests – or vice versa?

You may also have indirect competition – could your guests stay with friends or relatives, for example, rather than a hotel? Could they travel on the day rather than stay with you the night before their meeting? Could they have their wedding on the beach in the Seychelles rather than a traditional reception? What will your guests be prepared to pay for and see as value added when compared with this indirect competition?

Consider your price-sensitive services or products. What are the services or products you sell that your guests will use as their benchmark? You want to ensure you get a sale first, then upsell from there. If people perceive they are getting value for money on the core items, they are much more likely to spend on additional items.

Action 5.1 Review your own tariffs and pricing

How do your guests perceive your prices? How do your prices compare with other hotels targeting the same guest profile? What do you already offer that differentiates you from them and gives value for money from your guests' perspective? What can you offer which any indirect competition could never compete with? What else can you do simply to add value for money without lowering your prices?

Plan and cost your offers, deals and promotions

Before you launch any promotion, make sure you do your sums so you know your breakeven point. Then ensure you have the infrastructure in place to support the promotion.

A 20% reduction in your selling price on a 30% margin equates to a 66% drop in profit margin; and a 40% reduction in selling price at 30% margin means a **10% loss** on each sale. Sorry if this is too much like a maths lesson, **but you must know your numbers.**

With any promotion you conduct be sure you have

clear objectives. Most promotions will have the goal of bringing in more guests, but is this at a price and as part of a longer-term marketing strategy (remember that each guest has a lifetime value – what they will spend with you over time), or does it need to be profitable in its own right?

Promotions do not have to be costly. For example, you may have an oversupply of some particular stock, or you can purchase a particular product when in season for a very reasonable price. Or maybe your suppliers or joint venture partners are prepared to donate towards your promotion, if they are set to gain from it. Your promotion may help you to use some of your fixed costs, incurring very little additional cost. For example, whether you sell a bedroom or not you will still have fixed costs associated with that empty bedroom. For single occupancy you will incur some additional cost but for a double or even family occupancy your variable costs will not rise proportionately.

Be creative with your promotions – don't just copy what your competition is doing, as it won't stand out. Promotions need to stimulate activity; they need to give people an incentive to come and visit **you** so they need to be exciting, worthwhile and enticing enough that your guests and prospects feel compelled to try your hotel.

Make offers **personal** and **tailored**. Show you have really thought about your guests.

Try before you buy

Try before you buy is a great way of encouraging people to try something new or entice them away from another venue with no risk to them.

Here are just a few suggestions:

- **Taster evenings** for your new menu for your local neighbourhood or regular guests. You don't need to give a full-blown meal, just a sampling of different menu items. Although the food will be free, people will still be buying drinks. If you do this before your normal service times, it might also encourage people to stay on for a full meal.
- **Wine tastings**, particularly when you are changing your wine list. Your wine merchant might also provide some sponsorship for this.
- Invite local clubs, associations and business groups to use your **meeting facilities** free of charge for their first meeting.
- Invite representatives from your **local tourist information centre** to try out your facilities and experience what you offer first-hand. This means you will be the first venue to come to mind when asked.
- Invite front-of-house staff from **local tourist attractions** to sample what you have to offer so they can make recommendations to their visitors.
- Invite existing customers to **bring a friend**

with them for free (your existing customers are your best form of referral and by inviting them to bring a friend you are increasing the loyalty of the existing customer).

- Offer first **conference booking** free if they book a series of events.
- Invite social secretaries from local clubs to a **function menu tasting**.
- Invite **PAs and secretaries** from local businesses to a networking meeting enabling them to sample your meeting and conference facilities.
- Offer a lunch or dinner for four to potential **wedding parties**.
- Set up a **networking event** for local trades people enabling them to sample your food and meeting facilities, so they might refer you to their customers.

All these suggestions are an ideal risk-free way to give your guests and prospects confidence in what you provide. Even more importantly, this starts to build a relationship and loyalty towards you.

Action 5.2 Try before you buy

What services or offers could you offer as a try before you buy?

Inclusive deals and packages

Bundling a number of your services or products together is a great way to offer value for money, and encourages your guests to try something that they might not otherwise buy.

Don't be scared off by what, on paper, looks like a small margin when you cost everything in; the more you include in your offer the less likely it is that everyone will take up all parts of the offer. For example, even if you offer two nights' stay including dinner, bed and breakfast, afternoon tea, up to two free spa treatments, free entry to (specified local attraction), the chances are that most guests will only take up a proportion of these offers. The important thing is that you make the offer excellent value for money, irresistible to your target audience, and prompt a booking.

The permutations are almost endless, especially if you look beyond your own facilities and join up with partners. Here are a few potential deals and packages for you to get the ball rolling:

- Two nights B&B to **include dinner on your first night** – this encourages your guests to eat in the hotel and provide an increased spend on wines and spirits
- **Fixed-price** two or three course table d'hôte
- Stay any Tuesday or Wednesday night in February (or any quiet month) and get **afternoon tea included**
- **Gourmet weekend** to include two nights' bed

and breakfast, six-course dinner and pre-dinner drinks on Saturday night, use of all leisure/spa facilities

- **Murder mystery evening** with period costumes provided, including dinner, overnight accommodation and breakfast
- Eat in the restaurant on a Wednesday evening and receive a signed copy of **chef's latest recipe book**

Activity packages

Put together packages of everything guests need for an activity weekend or break.

This might include access to sporting facilities, and hire of equipment, maybe even personal tuition or coaching (as a joint venture with the appropriate club or venue).

- **Midweek fishing break** including two nights' B&B; fishing permit, bait and equipment hire; packed lunch; and dinner at choice of hotel restaurant or partner restaurant
- **VIP Day trip** to Six Nations rugby (or other big sporting event) including: full English breakfast before departure, transport to and from venue in executive coach, tickets to the event, three-course lunch in hospitality marquee, supper on return. This type of event appeals to your local customers as well as guests
- **Biking break** including mountain bikes or road bikes (either the hotel's own or hired from

your local bike hire shop), helmets, packed lunch or special deal with local pubs, planned routes and maps, highlighting places of interest on route

- **It's a Knockout** contest with local outdoor activity centre or stage your own if your grounds permit – invite local businesses and clubs to form their own teams – offer different types of packages with and without accommodation.

One-off activities unique to your hotel

Where you can, make your offers and promotions something only *you* can offer as a hotel.

Combine your unique spa treatments, your chef's special recipes or 'home made treats', a guide only your hotel offers, a wine only you stock – anything that your competition cannot specifically copy. Use your location, your team, your building, anything that is unique as a basis for a package or promotion.

- If your building has some **historical interest**, hold a themed period evening or weekend
- Tie up with local activities such as **flower shows**, **exhibitions**, **festivals** or **sporting events**, and offer vouchers to the organisers of the events to help with your promotion
- What do you supply in your hotel that guests love, for example personalised toiletries? Can you offer this as a free gift with every booking?

Action 5.3 Inclusive deals and packages

What inclusive deals and packages could you offer?

What activity packages?

What does your hotel have which is unique and could form the basis of an offer or deal?

Use your 'expert' topic to add a perception of value

We talked about how being an expert can help you define what you offer, and your ideal guests on page 44. Developing an expertise enables you to build rapport with a niche market of potential guests, and gives you an opportunity to run exclusive events and promotions for these customers' market, which they perceive as value for money.

As a starting point, you can host meetings or club/group dinners and general social events. To take the step further you could invite topic experts, celebrities or people of specific interest or host quizzes or workshops. This might provide another opportunity for a joint venture (see Chapter 10). For example, if your topic is gardening, you might be able to form a partnership with a local nursery, garden designer, gardening author, historical/ famous garden, manufacturer of garden products, or market gardener (or all of these).

To capitalise on your expert topic run educational weekends and breaks. These might include a combination of the above. Continuing gardening as an example, it might include talks from experts, transport and free entry to a number of local gardens of interest (maybe as exclusive guests of the owner), plant sales through a local nursery, special promotional prices on other garden products from manufacturers or wholesalers, menus planned around locally grown produce.

It's even better if you can tie in with any specific gardening events happening locally, such as RHS flower shows, Gardeners' Question Time, etc. Or host your own Gardeners' Question Time calling upon local gardening celebrities.

You could follow a similar theme for any specialist area be it spas, cars, food, fashion, sailing, singing, cheese making, wine tasting, archaeology, geology, and anything else you can think of.

Promoting this type of event is so much easier than general promotions as you have a specific audience who you know has a particular interest. And (importantly) if you share this interest, you are in a much stronger position to present things in a way that will appeal to your target audience. If you do not share this interest, then involve someone who does, who can totally relate to and empathise with your prospects and guests.

Action 5.4 Use your expert topic

How can you use your 'expert' topic to offer value for money?

Early bird offers

Give your guests an irresistible incentive to book in advance rather than leaving things to the last minute or on an ad hoc basis.

This way you have a better chance of securing the booking and it helps with your planning (and cash flow too if they pay a deposit.).

You might offer a special price for bookings made by a certain date, but you can be more creative with your early bird promotions:

- Order a picnic lunch the night before and get a **half bottle of wine** included
- Book your spa treatment on check in and receive a **voucher** for £10-worth of spa products, plus 25% off your second treatment
- **Free guide book** when you pay your deposit
- Book by x date and be entered into a **prize draw**
- Book for your Mother's Day lunch by end of February and receive a **bouquet of flowers** for Mum
- Book your weekend break more than 6 weeks in advance and get a **complimentary upgrade**
- Book your meeting room one month in advance and get **complimentary breakfast** on arrival

 Action 5.5 Early bird offers

On what service(s) could you offer early bird offers?

What incentives will you offer to the guest?

Upgrades

People often remark that once you have flown at the 'front' of a plane you'll never want to go back to economy! For hotels the same principle can also apply – so give people a taste for your best offers, services and products to encourage them to upgrade at their own expense next time around.

Upgrading also leaves guests with a better experience than they may have expected, which promotes a talking point and is a great way to prompt testimonials and get referrals.

You can offer upgrades on most of your items, not just rooms, for example:

- Get a **free evening meal** with a stay of 2 nights or more (effectively upgrading to half board)
- Pay for a continental breakfast when you book and **upgrade to our full English** at no extra cost
- Stay two or more nights and get a **free upgrade to a suite** or executive room (on

availability)

Depending on the services offered by your hotel, you could effectively upgrade on any of these in return for advance booking, longer stays, deposits paid, or anything else that helps you in some way. But it doesn't have to be conditional – offer an upgrade anyway on arrival if you know you won't otherwise let that room – this gives the guest something unexpected and special to remember you by and promotes goodwill and loyalty.

 Action 5.6 Upgrades

Where or when could you offer upgrades?

Teaming up with others

We'll discuss more on working with partners as joint ventures in Chapter 10, but for now let's just cover how these often provide ideal opportunities to offer better value for money.

Supplier promotions

Ask your suppliers what promotions they have scheduled for the year. Some of these may be perfect to pass on to your guests to give added value.

The obvious ones will be food and wine suppliers, but there may be other areas, too:

- Your **toiletries supplier** offering products as gifts (especially to coincide with Mothers' Day or Christmas)
- Your **wine supplier** for Fathers' Day, the arrival of a new wine from a celebrated vineyard, or end of bin offers
- Your **grocery supplier** on luxury items and hampers as gifts for guests, guest purchases, or as prizes for a competition or draw
- Your **local butcher** to offer special rates for guests on locally farmed meat that you serve in the hotel

You might also team up with your suppliers to run events, where they provide information, give demonstrations, and invite their customers to the event. For example:

- Your **florist** to run flower arranging workshops
- Your **baker** to give a bread making demonstration
- Your **greengrocer** to give information and a talk on organic gardening or growing your own vegetables
- If you buy your **toiletries** from a local supplier who makes them from their own ingredients (e.g. a lavender grower) to give a talk on the production process and qualities of natural ingredients, and put together an exclusive gift package for your guests
- Your **wine supplier** to host a wine tasting and off-sales of discounted wine and supply the wines for the dinner

- Your **accountant** to host a seminar on taxation.

Just think of anything that might be of special interest to your guests.

Joint promotions with local joint venture partners

Don't worry that these businesses may only attract locals – their customers will pass on your details and recommend you to their friends, relations and colleagues.

For example, your local hairdresser or beauty salon may have a client who is getting married and needs to find a venue, and places for her family to stay. A local business will have visitors with people needing accommodation. Your local cricket club may be holding an event and need a venue and accommodation for those who want a drink without worrying about the drive home.

Here are a few ideas to get the ball rolling.

- Stay any Saturday night in January (or your quietest month) and get two free top-price tickets for your **local theatre**, the **pantomime** or **attraction**. Run this as a joint venture with the theatre/attraction
- Team up with **local boutiques** for a fashion week (or month) to coincide with the arrival of new season stock, and staging fashion shows, exclusive shopping evenings and discount vouchers at the boutiques

- Gardeners' midweek spring package – arrange talks from a **local garden designer or nursery**; arrange a visit to local gardens of interest (where you have arranged minimal admission prices or free in return for an invitation to the hotel), arrange discount for your guests at specialist nurseries or plant centres
- Offer a pampering and beauty promotion as a joint venture with your **local salons, spa and hairdressers** – you provide guests with discount vouchers or – better still – include treatments in the price of the package. The salons in turn promote the hotel and your facilities, sending their customers to you.

Action 5.7 Joint venture opportunities

What opportunities can you identify to get together with others?

Suppliers?

Joint venture partners?

Offer money-back guarantees

Offering money-back guarantees reverses the risk to your guest in choosing your hotel.

If you are really confident about the quality of what you offer, you should not have any qualms about offering your guests a guarantee to demonstrate this. This is one thing that few of your competitors will be doing.

Not sure what you can guarantee? Here are some ideas. You can back up some of them with a guarantee that's not 'cash' based – a gift or upgrade, for example.

- The best wine list in town
- A friendly welcome
-  The best views of ...
- All breakfast ingredients have come from within a 10-mile radius
- The best steak and kidney pudding in ...
- The latest check-out in town
- A minimum of 10 choices at breakfast
- A quiet night

Whatever you are proud of and confident that you can deliver, put this on your guarantee list. It's a good idea to have a guarantee for one of your 'different' or 'unique' features – another reminder why people should stay with you.

Is this a risk? Not really. Some will be subjective, but few people will ever contest it, but even if they do, the odd refund is better than no sale at all.

Action 5.8 Guarantees

What guarantees could you offer your guests?

Do something exceptional

Finally, the best way to give your guests the perception of value for money is to give them something exceptional and unexpected.

You and your team need to recognise and capitalise on any opportunities to do something over and above what your guests expect – something that will be remembered and talked about when asked if they had a good stay in your hotel.

And this doesn't even have to cost you anything more than time and attention. Helping with a request, organising something needed, a small token gift, a handwritten card, a printed out map or information with personal recommendations – none of these is 'expensive' but in most cases would be unexpected and exceptional.

Chapter 5 recap

In this chapter we have covered:

- ✓ How to offer value for money
- ✓ Encouraging existing and prospective guests to try something new with **try before you buy**
- ✓ How offering your guests **special offers, deals, upgrades and promotions** adds value without giving discounts

- ✓ Using your **'expert' topic** to attract the attention of those who share your interest
- ✓ Opportunities to add value by **teaming up** with other businesses
- ✓ How to prompt and secure **advance bookings**
- ✓ Reassuring guests by giving **guarantees**

Authors' comments

Caroline: When I work with hotel and restaurant teams we get the best results when everyone gets involved. Staff love to have the opportunity to contribute their own ideas for adding value and in planning promotions (and most have some great ideas, too). Have a bit of fun with these, but remember to keep those numbers in mind, too.

Lucy: With all offers and promotions, make the most of them PR and marketing-wise. Promote them on your website, in social media and in the press. Write a blog post or article about your offer and **why** you're doing it. Every offer will have a story – being open, honest and explaining why you're running it can really make for interesting reading and set you apart from your competition (and help with bookings). I always encourage business owners to demonstrate the personality behind their business, and once they see the value it pays dividends.

Chapter 6

Market your hotel online

Chapter 6

Market your hotel online

Too many businesses build a great website, then just hope that everyone will find it.

Unfortunately it's not quite as simple as that. You could have what looks a fantastic website for your hotel, but hardly get a single visitor. So all that effort to create your website will be wasted.

There are **only two things** that you should have as goals for your hotel's website. The first is to **get more traffic** to your site – qualified traffic that is – visitors who fit your perfect guest profile. The second thing your website should be doing is **converting as many of these visitors into paying guests as possible**.

But first things first – let's look at ways to get more qualified traffic to your hotel website.

In this chapter, we explain how to:

✓ Use **pay-per-click** (PPC) advertising to bring more visitors to your website and track them

✓ Drive qualified traffic to your website from **other sources**

✓ Get your name, your expertise and your business known online by **writing articles**, **blogging** and using **social media**

Promote your website with advertising you can track

Pay-per-click (PPC) advertising brings qualified traffic to your website, is entirely measurable and you only pay for results (i.e. visitors to your site).

PPC works by you 'sponsoring' key phrases (the words that people type in to Google or another search engine) and then having your 'ads' come up in the search results (as text) when people search for those phrases. You don't pay every time your ad is 'seen' – you pay **only** when someone clicks on your ad to visit your website. So you're only paying for visitors to your website, not for general advertising. Compare this with a listing or a print advert, where you pay for the advertising no matter how many people then visit your website (which could be none).

Pay-per-click advertising is an excellent way to boost qualified traffic to your website as you're entirely in control of the key phrases (search terms) you target, and you can make these wholly relevant to your market.

PPC advertising is also great because you can track its success very clearly from search phrase – what someone types into Google, for example – right through to enquiry. So you know **exactly** which key phrases and ads bring in guests and which don't. This is where having goals set up in your Google Analytics comes into play (you can track which phrases convert to bookings or the enquiry form being completed for example).

So now you don't have to advertise and hope that your potential guests will see your ads without you knowing exactly what makes them enquire to stay with you. With PPC ads you **know** what they're looking for.

There is more to PPC advertising than just haphazardly writing some ads for Google Adwords (or another search engine) and adding in your credit card details. It **can** be a very easy way to spend a lot of money if you're not quite sure what you're doing. There is a learning curve in trying out different key phrases and adverts to see which ones do work for your audience and your hotel. So don't expect a perfect campaign from Day 1. Spend time on your campaign and closely monitor the results. When you can **really** see what is and isn't working you'll have a completely transparent campaign that drives people to your website and generates enquiries.

We recommend that you start by enlisting the help of an expert who will research, set up and manage your PPC campaign until it's at a stage where it's working well and you can easily maintain it. Even then, don't think you can rest on your laurels! The fast-moving nature of the Internet means that campaigns change all the time and different search terms become more effective.

Monitor what your competitors are doing (just searching for your own sponsored key phrases to see what the competing ads look like helps enormously). Also look at how effectively your website pages (and those of your competitors) convert enquiries to guests. It makes sense to manage your PPC campaign (or have someone manage it for you) on an ongoing basis, constantly evaluating and monitoring to ensure it's getting the best results for you. It's not something you should set up and leave if you want best results.

The advantages of PPC advertising are many. With PPC advertising you're always **100% in control of your budget** and your target audience – so whenever you want to stop or start a campaign or widen or narrow a search area (geographic or time of day or time of year) you can do this instantly. You can switch off and switch on PPC advertising when it suits you. So if you're full, say for Easter, you can switch off all your Easter-related ads the minute that happens so you're not wasting your marketing budget or generating enquiries that you can't handle. Whereas, if you only advertise for Easter offline (in print for example), then once your ads are printed they're printed and you're paying for them if you're booked up or not.

Use the results of your PPC campaign, too. It will give you great 'market research' and a deeper understanding of the key phrases and offers your guests respond to. Use these results across all your marketing and in your website. So if you notice that it's always three nights for two offers that get the most clickthroughs, promote these. If key phrases that use words like 'adults-only holiday', or 'sea view suites' get you new bookings, use these key phrases in your website to help boost your natural search results and use them in your print adverts and brochure. You've proved them to be the search terms that generate you business so make them as visible as possible.

Action 6.1 Trial and track pay per click

If you have budget available for online marketing PPC is a good way to have a measurable campaign.

Trial using PPC for one offer or set of keywords (destination/holiday type/service/seasonal offer).

If you're already using PPC – are you constantly reviewing and changing your ads? Are the keywords you are using a match to those you came up with in Chapter 3 (Action 3.11).

Drive traffic to your website from other sources

Links from other websites that also target your perfect guests are powerful sources of traffic, and help with SEO (search engine optimisation) to get you higher search engine rankings. And the higher your search engine result the more likely your site will be visited.

A joint venture – working with another business that is targeting the same audience as you (see Chapter 10) – is very easy to do online. And don't just think that you need to 'advertise' on related websites, as often there is a much better way to get results from their traffic.

Travel and entertainment websites can bring you more bookings. **Directories** can also work well, but think about which are most compatible or most targeted at your particular market. However, don't just list your hotel on every site that your competitors do because you feel you have to. You'll be able to see very easily which sites generate you traffic and enquiries from looking at your website statistics (see page 60).

On listings sites you do want to be in (that also feature your competitors), think how your hotel will stand out from all the others. Have a striking headline – or focus on a unique feature or type of holiday you offer. Don't just have the name of your hotel and a photo like everyone else – **make sure it's <u>your</u> hotel they click on!**

And don't forget to ask your guests which websites **they** use. You might be surprised what sites they look at regularly – for news, hobbies, sports. Find out where they spend time online and make sure you're there too.

Other ways to get people to your site

Posting on forums builds your reputation and gets you noticed. Capitalise on this by including links on any information you post online. Include your web address and email address in all mailings and all promotional material either online or offline.

Links in your printed material. Have a link to your website (or better still a specific landing page) to tie in with what you say offline. You may need to offer an incentive to get people to 'go online' (as when they're already online you're only a click away). A deal, offer or competition can help here.

Action 6.2 Find partner sites and forums

Use search engines to look for suitable partner sites that could bring you traffic – use the keywords and phrases your guests would use, and see what sites come up in the results.

Find a forum(s) that your ideal guests spend time on and pose questions and comment.

Write articles

Apart from advertising, which will cost you money, another way of getting your name known is by writing articles.

This is a lot easier on the Internet than it is in print, and you can contribute to many forums, other blogs and article sites at no charge.

Think about where your prospects will be looking online. As well as talking directly about your hotel or restaurant, use relevant sites to discuss or comment on your **expert topic**; this is a great way to get your venue recognised and talked about by your ideal guests. Whenever you can, include a link to your website.

Put your articles – or links to them – in:

- your own hotel blog (see below)
- online article sites and forums – these can be travel sites, or sites that focus on your expert topic or niche market (e.g. sports sites, interest sites, business sites, family sites)

- comments to other people's blogs
- guest blog posts
- in print wherever you can.

Start blogging

A blog (which is short for 'web–log') is a way of keeping your web presence up-to-date.

While blogs started out as 'online journals' they're now very much more than this. A blog allows you to showcase the personality of your business. The format of a blog gives individual writers the chance to share information, update readers (guests and potential guests) and be very timely. A blog is somewhere you can really go to town with detail or hot topics or your latest offer or update. And the good news is that search engines love blogs as they love up-to-date content.

Here are some ideas of what you can include in your hotel blog:

- News – about you, the hotel, your destination

- Menus and recipes
- Offers
- Latest thoughts and opinions – use latest news and trends as a basis for your own comments
- What's happening at the hotel
- What's happening in your area – events, shows, new restaurants, travel connections, leisure attractions, the weather.
- Contributions from staff
- Articles and discussions around your 'expert' topic

Blogs provide another opportunity to promote your hotel or restaurant, by telling your story and setting you apart from your competition. They enable you to show your personality and expertise, so you build a stronger relationship with your target audience.

Blogs are also fantastic for SEO (Search Engine Optimisation) as the search engines find new blog content to list much quicker than they do new content on a 'normal' website. For example, Google may only come and 'crawl' your main website every six weeks or so to see if there is anything new. But it crawls blogs all the time and it's entirely possible to get posts referenced in a couple of hours.

You can use your blog to talk about events and news in your area and use this as a 'piggy back' opportunity to promote your own hotel.

Example

> *A well-known band announces they're re-forming and will be playing a concert in your town. You know this band will appeal to your target guests, and (more importantly) they'll probably be searching for tickets and info online as soon as they hear the concert announced. You want to capture this traffic so you:*
>
> *Write a blog post as soon as the dates are announced, promoting concert packages, or two-night stays for the dates of the concert. If you put this offer up on your main website it might be weeks before the search engines find it. On your blog you'll be picking up searches for this concert the same day, and no doubt some bookings too.*

Blogs are also a great tool for starting discussions with your guests. This helps you gather more information for your guest profiling. Set up your blog to accept comments (although we strongly advise you set these up to be approved (or not) by you to eliminate spam and keep the discussions relevant.). Also it's a good idea to have an email subscription box on your blog (and very easy to do), so people can receive an email update from you each time you post a blog. This makes your blog work like a newsletter that people have opted-in to read.

To set up a blog we recommend using WordPress (www.wordpress.org) as the best platform. The software is free and while there are also free templates available for the design of your blog, it's a good idea to have a custom template designed to fit with your brand. It can also make a lot of sense to have your blog 'in' your website so it's easy for readers to link off to the rest of your site and make a booking.

A good web designer can make a WordPress blog 'look' exactly like the rest of your website so you can easily add this to your existing website.

The good news is that you don't then need a web designer to access and update your blog – it's easy to do with WordPress as everything is available from a browser and you just log in online. You can create new posts and pages as easily as if you were using a word processor. You don't need to know any code – all you need to do is type.

Don't make your blog a series of adverts or offers only, though – this isn't its purpose. Make your blogs informative, write them regularly and let your personality show through. You can also comment on other people's blogs to add to discussions or start your own. The chances are that the writer of that blog will then investigate yours, so it's another good way to make contact.

There are a lot of blogs out there on the Internet but if you make yours relevant, interesting and packed with information aimed at your ideal guest audience you will pick up traffic from online searches. It's quite feasible for someone to find your blog because they Googled a sport or hobby they have a keen interest in, and end up booking to stay at your hotel as a result. That's how you need to think – who do I want to stay at my hotel and what will they want to read about.

Action 6.3 Write articles and blogs

Start a list of all the topics you feel confident to write about on your blog or as articles:

about your area

about your holiday experiences

about events

about your expert topic

Find other blogs it would be good to comment on and join in – destination and travel-related or associated with your expert topic

Use social media

Social media sites such as Facebook, LinkedIn and Twitter are great ways to build your profile and credibility and drive traffic to your website and – ultimately – to your hotel.

LinkedIn

Use LinkedIn (www.linkedin.com) to connect with a more corporate market, and post articles through various forums and get known. LinkedIn should be a good place to look for joint ventures or other 'professional' partnerships, as it's very business-oriented. Make use of networks and connections you already have, and find new groups relevant to your target market by using the 'search groups' function on LinkedIn.

If your 'expert topic' is business-related and has a professional audience, LinkedIn is a great place to showcase this. Join in with questions, participate in groups, and keep your profile up to date.

Twitter

Twitter (www.twitter.com) is proving to be great source of partnerships and customers for many businesses, including hotels and restaurants. On Twitter you can post offers and create links – either to a sales page, your brochure site or a landing page. You're limited to 140 characters per message or 'Tweet' but you can still use this as a way of promoting links to your own and others' articles. Twitter is also proving to be a useful tool for advertising promotions.

That said though, the emphasis **must** be on social connections and business to make Twitter work for you. Businesses that are successful on Twitter are so because they have a person who tweets for them. Twitter is about interactions and conversations; it's not about selling. So be interesting, be funny, join in, and then it is acceptable to mention your offers and promotions without them being seen as 'in-your-face' advertising.

With all social media, but Twitter especially, think about it as a conversation you're having with someone, not a billboard. You'd never stand up in a room full of people you've never met before and announce – Hi! I'm the manager of the best hotel in Devon and we've got a 2 for 1 offer on this weekend; do you want to book?

You'd instead (we hope!) introduce yourself by name, mention that you're the manager of a hotel in Devon, have two kids, moved from London a few years ago, and that you have a really keen interest in horse riding. You may then go on to share that you love riding on the beaches near to you in Devon and then perhaps share some tips about your favourite locations for a canter. **Then,** if the conversation carries on (as by now you've worked out who it is that's interested in horse riding – your expert topic) you can mention you've got a special offer for riding holidays at your hotel where you take people out to your three favourite beaches for a great riding experience. **Now** you're more likely to get some bookings.

Build your credibility on Twitter first by giving some valuable information; forwarding ('retweeting') other's posts and gaining interested followers.

Ask your guests to join your network and join in online by sharing their experiences, asking questions or commenting with links to your blog.

Some hotels have a good Twitter profile – they share information about what the hotel offers – tweeting menus and breakfast items, activities their guests have been doing, and testimonials. At the same time though, you can always spot the 'corporate' tweeters from the 'real people'. If you want to stand out from your competition, establish yourself as an expert, and show off the personality of your hotel, make sure it's **you** doing the tweeting, or real people on your team who can also be personal. Twitter is you talking directly to your guests in a way they like to chat, so make the most of it, as there are lots of conversations out there waiting to happen.

Facebook

Like all social media, everything is 'real' and based on person-to-person recommendations in Facebook. It's essentially an online marketing channel, but you should try not to 'commercialise' how you use it too much – keep it human and it will work. You can run Facebook-only promotions and offers and engage your audience with competitions and other 'fun' things to get your name known. There is the option of establishing a business Facebook profile to separate your activity out from any personal account you may have. This also helps people to know that you will be talking about your business so there's no surprise there. A good idea with Facebook is to set up a 'Fan' page where you can showcase your offers and news, and bring together your other online marketing activity – your blog, your tweets and your articles for example.

If your ideal guests are using Facebook, you need to be there too. Social media sites are places people have chosen to spend time online, so make sure you're there if they are the audience you want. Remember that Facebook can work like one giant referral engine as people will make recommendations and follow what their friends are doing.

Where do your guests go online?

Social media sites are fast becoming a key marketing tool for reaching audiences where they're already spending time online.

Work out where **your** guests are spending time socialising online. The sites mentioned here are just examples, but there are lots of others. The key always is to be where your guests are.

Things to think about include your guests' interests, their ages, how much time they spend online, how they interact with their own friends and business colleagues. These will help you to identify where you need to 'be' in social media. You don't need to be on **every** community and list, but don't ignore this growing and powerful medium – there are **lots** of your potential customers out there using it.

Once you've decided which social media sites you want to be on, include your profile details as links (ideally use the logos associated with each site for instant recognition) so people can find you and 'connect' or 'follow' you easily. Add your social media profiles to your contact information on your website and printed materials.

Action 6.4 Find out where your customers go online

Ask them – when booking, feedback forms, in conversation.

Google their interests to see sites that come up

Look at printed media's online sites (newspapers, magazines).

Find online communities that reflect your ideal guest demographic and interests (mums' sites, business sites, sport sites, etc.

Look at social media sites to choose the best one for your hotel to engage on.

Finally, do remember to track your success with social media. It's very easy to spend a lot of your valuable time on this with no tangible results. Use Google Analytics (see page 60) to track how much traffic it drives to your site, and ask guests how they heard of you or your offers.

Chapter 6 recap

In this chapter, we've covered:

- ✓ Using **pay-per-click** (PPC) advertising to bring more visitors to your website and track them
- ✓ Driving qualified traffic to your website from **other sources**
- ✓ Getting your name, your expertise and your business known by **writing articles**, **blogging** and **social networking**

Authors' comments

Caroline: Beware. If you are new to social networking it can be addictive, as many of my clients remind me. Set some objectives, track your results and limit your time accordingly.

Lucy: Measuring the results from your online marketing is vital to getting the right mix for your hotel. It's very easy to track visits to and conversions from your website, but make sure you're asking guests too – on the phone and in person – where did you see us online? Just because they may have booked from your website you need to understand where they are 'seeing' you, too.

Chapter 7

Traditional marketing

Chapter 7

Traditional marketing

It's sometimes easy to forget, in the age of websites, email and social media, what we did before. But many of the traditional marketing methods are still great ways to get you and your hotel noticed.

Like **any** sales and marketing activity you do, it's always about what works for **your** market.

In this chapter, we show you how to:

- ✓ Get your hotel talked about in the **press**
- ✓ Promote your hotel on the **radio**
- ✓ Make the most of **printed materials**, such as flyers, leaflets, postcards and inserts.

Get press coverage

The more your hotel or restaurant is talked about in the press, the better.

It is an effective way of attracting new customers; it also reminds your existing guests to revisit you, by rekindling their interest in you. But you need to target your press coverage to the places where your prospects and guests will read it. This is called public relations (PR).

The obvious way to appear in the press is by writing a press release. The only problem is that everyone else does this too, so think of it from the editor's perspective – what makes a compelling and newsworthy article, one that will interest his or her readers?

Talk to the editors and journalists and find out what type of stories or articles they would like more of, and if there are any particular angles they're interested in. Readers generally respond better to something that the publication has written about you, rather than something you have written yourself. So whenever you do anything that is potentially newsworthy, tell your local newspaper or lifestyle-appropriate magazine and invite them along to the event.

Even if they don't attend the event itself, it may present an opportunity for you to be interviewed. Make sure during the interview that you mention the name of your hotel and include your website address. This way, even if the journalists won't let you include your telephone number or contact details at the end of the article, it will still be included somewhere to enable people to follow up.

Easy ways to have a story picked up by the media are to link it to something **topical**, for example responding to something that is already in the press; or to make your story **controversial**. Either way, think of your target audience and whether they'll empathise with your comments.

Then, when you get any PR, post clippings and links on your website to add to your credibility and reputation. Also mention it in your blog and social media sites to make sure no one misses out on your coverage. You've done the work, so make sure the reach of your PR efforts is as wide as you can make it.

Action 7.1 Identify press opportunities

What publications or newspapers do your customers read?

What events either past or future are newsworthy? Think of an angle – one point that will be different and interesting.

What press coverage have you already had that you can capitalise on?

Write an advertorial

The alternative to public relations (where a journalist will write up a story 'in their own words') is to write an 'advertorial'.

This looks like a factual article, but is something that you have written and paid to have included in a newspaper or magazine. You'll often see these in print with the heading 'advertisement feature'.

Because advertorials don't **look** like an advert they're far more likely to grab the reader's attention. The article could be about your hotel, but might also be something about a particular interest, hobby or your 'expert' topic.

Ensure, as with any advertising, that you'll get a good return on this investment by placing it in a key and targeted publication for your audience. It's easy to get 'sold' advertising like this, but you only really want it if it's going to generate you business. Also make sure you can measure if the advertorial worked. Use a unique web landing page or offer code in the advertorial so you can measure how many enquiries or bookings it generated.

An alternative is to try this method online first, by featuring an article on another website (paid or free) or writing some 'guest' blog posts.

Action 7.2 Write an advertorial

Write down ideas for advertorial features, such as travel features or expert features

Write up an advertorial article you can place in printed media

Get on the radio

Being interviewed by a radio station is a great way to get your name and your venue talked about.

What do you do or have that is a worthy talking point? What have you already defined as your point of differentiation? Maybe you have an unusual event coming up in the future that may be of local or national interest? Having an expert topic (see page 44) may provide the perfect opening for a radio interview, too.

And once you have the interview – promote the recording. Have an audio file on your website and promote your interview in your blog. Chances are high many of your potential audience won't have caught your interview so make sure they can listen to it and don't be shy about promoting it. Often it's enough to have had the interview to establish your credibility even if no-one listens to it! But you have to let them know about it in the first place.

Action 7.3 Prepare a radio interview

Make a list of topics you'd like to speak about – make notes and have some case studies ready.

Approach radio stations that have shows which cover your topics.

Record an audio file (or a few!) to have on your website of you being interviewed on your topics so you have examples ready. The interview can be you/member of staff, but it means you've got more content for your website and an example for radio stations.

Use print inserts instead of on-page ads

A loose-leaf insert is far more likely to be read, as it's physical, and falls out into the reader's hands. Most magazines limit the number of

inserts that go into any one issue, so this alone gives them a higher profile.

Advertising in your local paper or community magazine may be a cost-effective method to get your venue known locally. But most people only skim the paper and once the paper is out of date it will quickly go in the bin.

An insert also outlives the magazine or paper – people who are interested will hang on to it, maybe pin it to a notice board, until a time when they're looking for a place to eat, or somewhere for relatives to stay.

With national publications, you can often target only certain regions or geographic areas with inserts, not the whole mailing list or country. This can be a good way to test the effectiveness of an insert. If you've found a publication you think will be right for your target audience, you can test one region at a lower cost and then, if it is successful, roll out to the entire mailing list.

Make sure your insert has a clear **offer** or **call to action** –make it clear what you want people to do next (remember AIDA, covered in Chapter 4). If you want them to visit your website set up a tailored landing page (see page 83). This way you can closely track the results of your campaign. The same goes for giving a phone number or offer as the call to action – have a code or way of identifying each publication or insert people respond to and record this to measure the success of your campaigns. To make your marketing budget work as hard as possible, you need to know what is and isn't working for you.

Action 7.4 Plan print inserts

If your ideal guests read printed publications:

Make a list of offers you can promote in an insert.

Write out headlines, calls to action and offer details.

Design a flyer or insert and test this in a targeted publication (by region if it's a large subscription base).

Do a leaflet drop

If you want to target people in your local area for a particular promotion, event or new offer – such as your latest menu – use a leaflet drop through the letterbox of your target audience.

Although not as personal as a letter or email, this can be effective. Limited to your direct local audience, it gives you an opportunity to tailor your message accordingly.

Make sure your offer:

- is clear and specific
- is tailored to your audience
- has a clear call to action
- is measurable – by directing readers to a specific landing page (for example) and includes a code to quote.

If you can, try and collect email addresses at the same time using a response form, or ask for it to send out any confirmations.

Action 7.5 Prepare a leaflet drop

Generate ideas for a local offer.

Design a leaflet with a clear call to action for your offer.

Target your leaflet by area, or postcode.

Measure response with a code or landing page.

Use direct mail

Sending letters, brochures, flyers and postcards is not dead. They're a great way to drive traffic to your website, generate direct enquiries, and establish professional relationships.

Direct mail is also important if your target market is not 'IT savvy' (for example an older age group). It does cost money, but a printed flyer, postcard or brochure has longevity. Your customer can refer back to it when the time is right. Even the most 'online' among us still like receiving nice things in the mail from the postman!

Postcards are a cost-effective way of communicating with your guests. They're more eye-catching than a letter, and more convenient to file (or better still stick on the fridge door) than a brochure or leaflet. Also think about when you can use postcards as part of continuing communications with existing guests. A tongue-in-cheek 'wish you were here' postcard sent in the summertime when they haven't visited you at that time of year before can work well. Or what about a Christmas card or Happy New Year card showing your hotel 'all decked out' to entice usual summertime guests to spend their festive season with you?

Direct mail pieces can be more successful than press advertising for driving people to your website. People often read them when they have access to their computer, and they're easy to 'file' or keep until they next log on to their computer. Your prospective guest can take the postcard or letter over to their computer, type in your address and go right to your site.

With direct mail advertising or articles about you in the local paper or magazine there may well be a lag between the time that prospects read your ad or article and the time they log in to your website (if they remember to at all). That's when it makes sense to have a ready-printed piece that's easy to keep hold of until they are online. Better still, make the call to action even more immediate by providing a free phone number to call or text option so the person doesn't even have to be online.

With direct mail you will need to take account of your print layout, design, proofing and printing, so allow enough time to set this up. Most printers will need your 'artwork' as a high resolution file, so unless you have the skills and the software to create these, you will need to find a graphic designer to help. Some printers may be able to do your artwork too, but remember if they are printers first and designers second this may not give you the finished result you are looking for in keeping with your brand image. Be aware, though, that often printers will make a small additional charge for checking your artwork if not created by them.

Here's a checklist of things to consider for any printed material. To minimise changes (and keep costs down), map all this out before briefing your designer:

- What is your **objective**? This may be to drive traffic to your site, gather contact details or make a booking, but be clear on this and have this in mind throughout
- Create your message – remembering **AIDA** – **A** an eye catching headline to grab their attention, **I** a compelling benefit to the reader to maintain their interest, **D** the details to create desire, and **A** your call to action
- What **layout** will you use? This will depend on the size of the finished article – postcard, A5 flyer, A4 letter, etc
- If using an **image** ensure this is in keeping with your identity – preferably your own photo as opposed to a stock photo
- What **format** does your printer require? e.g. PDF

- What **weight and finish** of paper do you need? For postcards you will need a heavier paper – your printer should be able to advise
- **How many** do you need? – Note some printers can provide digital printing, which may be more cost effective if you only require small numbers (tens or hundreds).
- Check **turnaround times** and **delivery dates** from the printer

Proof read everything and ask others to check too (a good tip is to read it backwards to pick up any spelling mistakes). This is your responsibility, not your designer's or printer's.

Action 7.6 Conduct a direct mail campaign

Draft direct mail letters or postcards

Test to a sample of your database

When you have a result you're happy with – roll out to your entire database, or with a partner to their database.

Chapter 7 recap

In this chapter, we've talked about:

- ✓ Getting your hotel talked about in the **press**
- ✓ Promoting your hotel on the **radio**
- ✓ Making the most of **printed materials**, such as flyers, leaflets, postcards and inserts

Authors' comments

Caroline: Avoid the 'scatter gun' approach. I often see hotels wasting time and resources with marketing material with no real plan of attack or strategy. With every piece of marketing you do, plan what exactly you want it to achieve, which will influence the medium you use, your timing and the message. Don't forget that your hotel team are also a form of marketing materials – by this I mean almost literally that they are walking, talking advertisements for you. Make sure they know all your literature, and convey the message to your guests that you'd want them to.

Lucy: It's very easy these days to get carried away with all the 'new' ways of marketing your hotel, but please don't forget there are still lots of other ways to communicate with your guests. As ever, it's about finding the best methods to connect and making sure you're not putting all your marketing eggs in one basket! That said – do make sure everything works together ('integrated marketing') so mention your website and social media sites in your traditional media and vice versa (e.g. promote your brochure and press clippings online).

Chapter 8

Build your guest relationship

Chapter 8

Build your guest relationship

People are more likely to buy from people they know, like and trust. Establishing a relationship with your guests and prospects enables this to happen, and in time turns to loyalty.

Relationships are built up over a period of time, but can be lost in an instant, which is something you need to be constantly aware of.

This section will enable you to:

- ✓ **Get to know** your guests, their likes and dislikes
- ✓ **Reward** your loyal guests to keep them coming back for more
- ✓ Show your guests you **listen** and **respond** by offering what they want and need
- ✓ Maintain your guests' interest by constantly offering something **fresh**
- ✓ Get your guests **doing the selling for you** by promoting your hotel to their friends and colleagues

Get to know your guests

Be there – your personality is part of the business

Being visible in your establishment and making personal contact with your guests builds rapport and trust.

But being visible is only half the story. What are you doing to reflect and convey your values and attitude to guests and staff? The way you interact with your staff and participate in the operation gets noticed.

Talk to your guests. This is by far the best way to get feedback. They may tell you things that they wouldn't feed back to your staff. Get to know your guests personally - their likes and dislikes, their routine, their suggestions, their network - all this not only builds rapport, but makes it a lot easier to upsell and tailor your offers to your market.

Why negative feedback is just as important as good feedback

Every bit of feedback you get from your guests is valuable to you, whether it's positive or negative and whether you agree with it or not.

Capture the good and the bad. If you don't agree with the feedback, find out (tactfully) what has led to their perception, as this may lead to the root of the problem. If you don't know what disappoints guests, you can't improve on it, so make sure you are prepared to listen to, and take on board any thoughts on what lets you down, so you can learn from this and address it.

Also identify **what factors would encourage them to return**. If certain services or facilities are important to this guest, the chances are they will be important to others, too. Also take note of the language your guests use to describe what they like. Capitalise on this information and use it in your marketing.

Consider the best way to get guest feedback. Few people like to fill in questionnaires, except maybe when they're really unhappy about something. Questionnaires can help you rectify your mistakes, but they often dwell on negatives rather than positives. So think how else you can capture feedback.

The best way is face-to-face, but it needs to be something a little more than:

> *"I hope you enjoyed your meal"*
>
> *"How did you enjoy your stay?"*

...which tend to give a very superficial reply. Think of some more direct questions such as:

> *"What did you enjoy the most?"*
>
> *"What was the best part of your stay here?"*
>
> *"If there was anything we could improve on, what would it be?"*
>
> *"I notice you had the seabass tonight. How was it?"*

Whatever format you use, make it user-friendly and show them that you appreciate the feedback. Then make it clear you've acted on it (even tell the guest).

Network in the right circles

Help to build rapport by taking the opportunity to meet with your guests or prospects in other environments, too.

Recognise that networking is not necessarily about meeting only with your guests directly. Much of the networking you do will be getting you in front of people who are able to influence your potential guests.

Too many people give up at the first hurdle of a networking meeting, complaining that they have not met any potential customers. Often your potential guests are already other peoples' customers, so always think about that, too.

Consider if it is your guests you want to meet, or the actual buyers or decision-makers – the 'bookers' we described in Chapter 1 who will be picking up the phone or logging in to make the bookings. Where do **these** people meet, socialise, or network?

Building rapport and trust takes time, so be prepared to invest some time and effort. Networking is about giving as well as receiving, so look for opportunities to help, either through referrals, information, or contacts.

And remember that a lot of networking is done **online** today – see page 158 to find out how social media can help you build your network.

Action 8.1 Get to know your guests

What else can you do to get to know your guests better?

In what ways can you get feedback from your guests?

What can you do to raise your visibility with guests?

What networking events or forums are there where your target guests meet? Or where their contacts meet?

Reward loyalty – it will reward you with profit

Recognition

The very least you can do is to remember your regular guests.

Capture their details and preferences – do they like a particular room, prefer a specific table or need a special pillow? Remembering these small details can make your guest feel valued.

Loyalty programme

Why do so many supermarkets, petrol stations and coffee shops give you loyalty cards? Because they work. Think about what you can do as a hotel to reward loyalty.

It can be as simple as a card that guests get stamped each time they visit. Ensure that any bonuses awarded are high value to your guests and qualifying levels are within their reach. But also ensure the rewards level is such that it promotes sufficient business (and profit) and does not diminish your margin in one hit.

To gain the best from your rewards scheme, capture your guests' personal details, so you add them to your list. Then let them know what each promotional offer is worth to them in points, to encourage them to spend and add to their points. The nearer they are to achieving a rewards level, the more tempting your offer will be, so if you have the facility to let them know their existing 'credit', so much the better.

You might offer special deals exclusively to those in your loyalty programme. These give them an automatic perception of scarcity, and so prompt attention. They are a good way of rewarding loyal guests and encouraging them to keep buying from you to accumulate their points or rewards.

Give your guests incentives to keep spending by offering progressively better value rewards the more they spend.

Monitoring their rewards levels does not have to be complicated – just a simple card that gets stamped can be all you need. But keep a track of people's rewards levels, so you can remind them when they are nearing a reward threshold to encourage them to visit or spend more.

Your rewards need to suit your target audience – something that is of real value to them or regarded as special. If your guest's bill is normally paid by a third party (e.g. business expenses) make the offer something they can benefit from personally – otherwise there is little incentive. Here are some reward ideas:

- Bring a guest for free
- Free upgrades
- Free weekend break
- Extra night free
- Exclusive use of special guest facilities, e.g. 'members' lounge',
- VIP access to special events
- Members' access to joint venture sports facility
- Offering 'secret' or special items not available to other guests
- In fact, any 'special deal' can be applied as an incentive for loyal guests.

Qualifying for a reward or thank-you may depend on something other than just their spending level. How about acknowledging guests who:

- Give you glowing testimonials
- Follow you on Twitter and RT (retweet) your messages
- Refer you to others
- Give you names and contact details of potential guests?

Remember their special diary dates

Why not help your guests to celebrate? Capture their birthdays and anniversaries on your database, and then invite them to the hotel to receive their special gift or offer.

- Invite wedding couples back for their first (and subsequent) anniversary.
- Make birthday cakes as a surprise to give a day to remember.
- Invite businesses to celebrate any awards.
- Keep a note of special anniversaries for local businesses – their AGM, awards dinners, anniversary of their launch.

People don't normally celebrate alone, so these provide ideal opportunities to bring in new guests. Make your offers worthwhile to encourage people to bring their friends or colleagues and make up a big party.

Receiving a birthday card with a voucher – or an invitation to celebrate a forthcoming anniversary – is a pleasant surprise, and adds a very personal touch. If you can hand write these, even better (it can make a huge difference and really demonstrate your interest in your guest).

Action 8.2 Reward guest loyalty

What could you do to reward guest loyalty?

Show you listen to your guests

Anticipate their needs

Demonstrate real guest focus by anticipating their needs.

Use the information from Chapter 1 to identify the things that will be important to different guest groups, e.g. speed and efficiency may be a priority for business users, whereas for families equipment for infants and small children (and staff who look happy to see them!) may be the number one priority.

Offer alternatives

Give your guests choice. This does not mean having 100 items on your breakfast menu or 40 types of pillow – but do give them a choice you can cope with.

In your restaurant, serving huge portions may be appealing to some, but others may be put off having a starter or dessert if they think the portion sizes are too big. Why not provide a taster version, for a slightly lower price, to ensure the sale?

Can you offer a choice of rooms in terms of features or facilities? Even if the rooms are all a standard layout, can you offer people a choice of outlook, proximity to reception, in-room amenities etc?

Can you be flexible to allow later check-outs (for an additional cost or as part of a promotional special) so guests have the opportunity to make the most of their last day before they head home? Do you have one room, which is very special in its own right, or where you can include extra services?

What else can you add to your standard offer to make a deluxe version to sell at a premium price?

Be flexible

You can't bow to every request a guest ever makes. But don't be so bound by the rules that any request is met with a hostile 'jobsworth' attitude!

If you cannot meet your guests' initial requests, look at offering an alternative:

- A guest wants an early breakfast, before your kitchen staff normally arrive – offer a continental breakfast or a tray instead.
- You receive a request just 10 minutes before service for an alternative to the set menu for a big party – you don't have a choice, but listen to what the guest needs to avoid and offer an alternative combination without this item.
- Your guests ring ahead and say they haven't been able to get a dog sitter. You don't take dogs, but can you find a local kennel to take Fido?
- Your guest asks for a particular brand of whisky for an important client he is entertaining. You don't stock it, so do you refuse, or phone your neighbouring hotel or pub to see if they have it in stock?

Overcome your guests' challenges

Think of other services you can provide that might just tip the balance in favour of that night out or weekend away. Think of the challenges your guests face, and how easily you could solve their problems:

- No baby sitter – offer babysitting
- What to do with the dog – recommend kennels (or allow dogs)
- Poor transport network – provide a free taxi service to and from the station or airport
- The kids will want their bikes, but we don't have a bike rack – offer bike hire
- We'll be bored if the weather is bad – set up a kids' play room and indoor entertainment area
- I don't have time to do my laundry – provide a laundry and pressing service
- I don't have time to get my legs waxed – give complementary vouchers for your own spa or a local beauty salon

See how these 'problems' offer great opportunities for additional services. The same goes for special occasions, learning a new skill or finding out if a new hobby appeals. Often we want an 'easy' answer – what to do for this occasion; how can I see if I like... I've always wanted to try...

Without having to think too hard or spend too much, people can have a ready-solved problem if you've put together a package 'just for them'.

Cater for special diets and needs

Catering for special diets and needs is the sort of attention to detail that builds you loyalty and referrals.

Let your guests know in advance if you can provide special diets or meals. The obvious one is catering for small children and babies if you want to attract families with children. Even if this is not your specific market, but to ignore children would be disadvantageous to your business, ensure you have something suitable for them. It's easy to stock up on organic baby food and snacks to have in your store cupboard, and you'll impress many grateful parent guests.

According to research by Coeliac UK, the hospitality industry is missing out on an estimated £1 million a year by failing to provide safe, gluten-free options, because sufferers feel obliged to eat at home. And this is just for the 1% of the UK population who have the disease.

Add this to the huge numbers who have some kind of allergy or intolerance to certain foods. If you don't cater for them, it's not just their custom you will lose – their whole party will probably end up going somewhere else.

You just have to look at any of the big supermarkets and their range of 'free from' products to recognise there is a huge market here.

Demonstrating a good understanding of any diet based on medical conditions is important if you are to instil any confidence with your diners. You must brief your staff and make sure they understand what could happen if they get it wrong. A dish containing 'just a little' of an ingredient to which the guest is allergic could be lethal.

To find out more about catering for special diets, see our website www.HotelSuccessHandbook.com for a list of resources.

Be sensitive to your guests' values

We discussed knowing your guest on page 19, but there will be times when your guests express specific values or preferences, and these can change over time.

An example might be **sustainability**. Your guests are probably becoming more conscious of sustainability, and if they prefer or expect your hotel to demonstrate sustainable practices, you need to be able to respond to this, or at least treat it sympathetically.

Offer other products and services

Be innovative in identifying other items to sell to your guests – before, during and after their stay.

What is there that makes your establishment or offer unique, that they might want to take home or share with others? Could you offer any of the following as additional sales?

- Convert your renowned menu or signature

dishes into a recipe book.

- Package your hand-made petit fours into a gift box to take home
- Offer birthday or celebration cakes for guests or diners celebrating special occasions
- Offer a hand-tied flower bouquet for anniversaries or special occasions
- Sell your homemade bread, marmalade or other preserves and chutneys
- Offer your finest ingredients as an off sale – cheese, meat, eggs, etc., if there is something special about them – locally sourced, organic, etc.
- Sell luxurious bathroom accessories, robes with your logo, and toiletries
- Do you get asked about your unusual crockery? Why not get in more stocks and sell that or make arrangements with your suppliers for direct home delivery?

All these provide a potential source of additional sales, a novelty value and that personal touch. Not to mention a great talking point from which referrals may well flow.

Sell gift vouchers

Gift vouchers are an easy product to sell online or on site. They provide an opportunity for a sale, and, if given to someone who has never been to you before, they are a like a referral, but even better as you are almost guaranteed a new customer.

Gift vouchers are also great for your cash flow, as they will be paid for at the time of purchase, often way before they are redeemed. To help you keep track, put a time limit on the voucher with an expiry date (but make sure this is clear to the buyer and the recipient).

Action 8.3 Respond to your guests' wants and needs

What do you need to do to respond to guests' wants and needs?

What don't you provide currently that guests have requested?

Where do you need to provide greater flexibility to meet guests' needs?

What particular challenges stand in the way of your guests making a booking?

What special diets do you get requests for? What do you need to do to get started on these?

What values do your guests have that need to be reflected in your operation?

What other products or services could you provide before, during or after their visit?

Do you sell gift vouchers, and if not what needs to happen to make these available?

Don't take your guests for granted

Never, EVER get complacent about either your guests' interest or about what you offer. Continually review your level of service and offering, make changes where necessary, and keep things fresh and interesting. You can't afford to stand still.

Then make sure you tell your guests what you are doing. In addition to your online and offline marketing activities there are plenty of opportunities to reinforce your message on site to your existing and potential guests.

Promote events

Let your guests know what you've got coming up in the future. Even if they won't be there to take advantage of it, it may prompt a return visit or they may pass the details on to others who might be interested in the event.

As well as advertising these events on boards or posters, consider flyers or leaflets that people can take away as a reminder, or pass on to friends and colleagues.

Ensure any promotional material is visible and eye catching – no point having it tucked away out of view. What are your high traffic areas – by reception, entrance to the restaurant, in lifts?

Seasonal offers or promotions

Sometimes you will run promotions at times when there is a lot of demand, but inevitably a lot of competition too. The key with these is to plan ahead.

Because your guests know that lots of other places will be offering deals you need to ensure there is a real incentive to book early (see early bird offers, page 135, for more ideas) so you can secure a booking.

You also need to offer something different from your competition. What will make your offer stand out above the rest? What will be attractive to your target audience?

- **Easter** for the family market – include children's Easter egg hunt, and other fun family activities (with indoor options, just in case).
- **Christmas** – decide if your audience want the traditional fare or really want to get away from the norm with an alternative Christmas lunch or party
- Can you help guests with their **Christmas preparations**? – Party organisers get a free turkey, a hamper, case of wine or gift voucher for your local butcher or wine merchant (as a joint venture with your suppliers)
- **Summer holidays** – what activities and entertainment can you include for even the wettest summer's day (organised on site or as

a joint venture with local venues), or what can you offer for those lovely sunny days?

- **Mother's Day** – include a very special personalised gift for Mum that others can't copy – handmade or branded will make gifts unique.
- **Father's Day** – with some activity or entertainment suitable for Dad (suitable for his age group and interests), which has to be pre-booked – to prompt advance bookings.

Promotion of the month

If your guests get to know that you feature different things each month this gives them an incentive to check you out to see what you have on offer this month.

Even if they are not interested in the actual offer, this might still be enough to get their booking. If not, it keeps you in their mind and gives you a reason to keep in touch:

- **Wine of the month** – buy two glasses and get the rest of the bottle free
- **Featured wine region** (or food region) of the month – 15% off all wines (dishes) from the region – ask your wine merchant or suppliers to sponsor this
- Your restaurant could feature different **seasonal ingredients of the month** – e.g. make a point of dishes including locally grown asparagus in June, strawberries in July, raspberries in August, chilli dishes in

September, and so on

- Base your promotion around **unusual seasonal or special events** – pick something your competitors won't be doing. There are lots of local events, or religious festivals and celebrations you could promote throughout the year. Or what about celebrating the 'national days' of other countries as a theme – Australia Day in January, 4th July for an America theme (both have good food and wine opportunities.)
- For all **monthly promotions**, draw up a schedule in advance so you can ensure variety with your themes and what's on offer
- **Film of the month** – or film genre, or film producer. Do something different with your in-house movies (even if you do this on DVDs). If you catch guests' attention with a Bond movie month, or Musicals month you're doing something different to your competition that may secure you a booking (providing you hold a DVD concierge licence)

Competitions and prize draws

Competitions and prize draws can be a good way of building rapport and goodwill with your existing guests.

And, as we discussed in Chapter 4, you can attract the attention of prospects with little or no risk to them, while building your list in advance for future promotions and offers.

- Use your **joint venture** partners too – to help

promote your competition, and maybe to provide or sponsor prizes.

- Attend [...] **event** and be entered for our prize draw to win £[...]-worth of vouchers for (e.g. wine, plants – whatever appeals to your guests)
- Send in **recipes** (or similar) for chef to choose new dishes – winner gets a dinner for four featuring the guest's recipe on the new menu
- Name the new **restaurant** and win £200 vouchers to use in the hotel
- Book a **Christmas party** by [date] and enter prize draw for a special Christmas hamper (including lots of your hotel's unique goodies such as home-made Christmas pudding made to chef's special recipe, or hand-made chocolate truffles)
- Come for **lunch** Monday to Thursday (or any specified time frame) and be entered into a prize draw for your chef to cook a four-course dinner in their own home for up to six people
- If you are a family hotel, sponsor a **school competition** or set up your own on a theme that attracts attention to the hotel – it could be as simple as a colouring or painting competition based on a local landmark or related to a feature of the hotel

Many of these ideas include something from the hotel as the prize. This adds further value to what you offer, and ensures that winners at least will have a first-hand experience of the hotel and a memento after the event to show or share with others. This creates goodwill and loyalty and a greater chance of further business, either directly or indirectly.

For any type of competition or draw, make a big feature of the **prize giving**, inviting competitors, sponsors, local guests and press for further exposure.

Action 8.4 Maintain your guests' interest

What events or activities could you organise to maintain your guests' interest?
Forthcoming promotions?
Promotion of the month?
Seasonal events?
Competitions or prize draws?

Get your guests to do the selling for you

Give people a reason to talk about you

There's nothing like a testimonial to endorse your hotel or restaurant. Pick up any research on advertising effectiveness and you'll see word-of-mouth at the top of the list.

Many people are likely to be influenced having read testimonials from other guests.

One of the best things about word-of-mouth is it is essentially free. But word-of-mouth can be slow and people are far more likely to tell other people about bad experiences than about good ones.

So how do you get people talking about you, and how do you get referrals? They won't say good things about you unless you meet and exceed their expectations. First, **do something exceptional**. Think of the things that are of high value to your guests but low cost to you so you can give added value. Give people a reason to talk about you.

Then **ask** for the testimonial. Ask for a comment in the guest book, on email, or on a review site. People need to be prompted to do this.

Get referrals

Referrals are a great way to build your customer base – if a person comes to you as a result of a referral, you don't need to go out

and find them.

The person who made the referral has already experienced what you offer and will do the selling for you.

Referrals build loyalty with the people who recommend you – they will want to be seen to stand by their referral by continuing to come to you themselves.

But referrals won't always happen unless you ask for them.

The obvious people to ask for referrals are your existing guests. Focus on those guests or customers who are your 'perfect guests' as the people they refer will be a better match to your preferred type of guest.

Think about other people who know you well enough to recommend you. This might include colleagues, suppliers, your own team and others in your network. This will be easier the better they know you and when they fully understand the extent of everything you offer.

Make the referral process easy

If you don't ask you don't get. So ask guests directly who else they know who may be interested in your promotions.

The sooner you do this after they have stayed or visited, the better. This is the time they are likely to be most positive about what you delivered.

The way you ask for referrals is key. If you ask:

> *"Do you know anyone who might be interested in receiving details of our promotions?"*

you are likely to get

> *"No"*

or at best

> *"I'll think about it."*

But if you ask a specific question, for example:

> *"Who else do you know who is celebrating [their birthday, wedding anniversary, retirement ...] in the next few months and may be interested in our [all-inclusive weekend breaks, wine promotion...]?*

Creating a simple referral form that you include with the bill can encourage existing guests to make referrals. Make this prominent, and offer incentives for them to give you names.

Maintain relationships with your guests, even if the likelihood of more business with them is limited. They are more likely to refer you to friends, colleagues or others if they have had recent communication from you.

Even if a guest only stays with you once they have a network of friends and colleagues who may also be your ideal guests. The lifetime value of one guest can be their connections to other guests, too.

Reward referrals

Encourage guests to give you contact details of others and referrals by rewarding them in some way.

As an absolute minimum, ensure that you thank anyone who makes referrals to encourage them to continue to do so in future. Don't wait to see if this actually leads to business, as what you are looking to reward is the referral process. The more referrals you have the greater the likelihood of gaining new guests.

Consider what other tangible incentives you might give that are of high value to the person making the referral, but at a low cost to you. Just ensure that the cost of the incentive does not outweigh the value of the referral. The nature of this incentive will obviously depend on where the referral came from, but they might include such things as a gift, cash bonus (to staff making referrals), discount off their next meal, an invitation to an event, or any of the ideas mentioned in *Building your list*, page 106.

Once you have a referral system in place, keep track of where and how you're getting successful referrals. This will enable you to find out what works and what doesn't, so you can refine the process.

Action 8.5 Get your existing guests selling for you

> How can you get your existing guests selling for you?
>
> What do you do that demonstrates exceptional service and will prompt guests to talk about you?
>
> What system do you have in place to gather referrals?
>
> What else do you need to do to get referrals?
>
> How do you reward people who give you referrals?

Chapter 8 recap

In this chapter we have covered:

- ✓ The importance of getting to know your guests, their likes and dislikes
- ✓ How to reward your loyal guests to keep them coming back for more
- ✓ How to show your guests you listen and respond by offering what they want and need
- ✓ Maintaining your guests' interest by constantly offering something fresh
- ✓ Getting your guests doing the selling for you by promoting your hotel to their friends and colleagues

Authors' comments

Caroline: It doesn't take too long to spot the hotel manager who is so focused on the numbers that they tuck themselves away back of house, never to be seen by their guests (or staff). I've worked with a fair few in my time. Whether this is down to time, lack of confidence, or even fear of what they'll find, once they see for themselves the benefits of getting out and talking to guests (and seeing things from the guests' perspective), few revert back to their old habits of hiding away in their office.

Lucy: Always, always remember that you need to find out what your guests want, and not assume that you know what that is. You must always ask your guests what they want, and act on the results. Remember your guests are a very valuable marketing resource for you.

You can also never assume you'll know what marketing will 'work' to attract the guests you want so you need to be testing, measuring the results, and making changes to your plan all the time. A good marketer knows that there is no 'right' answer, but everything needs to be tested and monitored – you do more of the things that work and keep on improving them.

Chapter 9

Involve your team

Chapter 9

Involve your team

Unless you are the only person who is going to come into contact with your guests, it's critical that everything you know about increasing sales you pass on to your team.

This section will enable you to:

- ✓ Identify what to look for when **recruiting** a team that can contribute to your hotel's success, and what you need to do to **attract good staff** in future
- ✓ Recognise how **training** is a must for good guest service, and why **systems and procedures** are important
- ✓ Identify **what training** is needed, and how every member of your team has a **part to play**
- ✓ Plan what training is needed to help you **increase spend per head**
- ✓ Identify ways to **encourage and motivate staff** to sell for you

Recruit the right people

Superstar staff will make all the difference to your hotel. In general, the people who will come in most contact with your guests are the

lowest paid. But these are the people who can make or break your business, so recruit the best you can afford.

You don't have to pay them an arm and a leg, but ensure that you at least offer a package that will attract and retain good people.

Be clear about what you are looking for. You can teach people how to take a reservation, serve wine, or clean a room. But it is far more difficult to teach someone to be warm, friendly, eager to please, courteous, discreet, use their initiative, or stay calm under pressure. It's even more difficult to instil your values on people. You need people who have a passion for the business and for guest service.

It is not only your front of house staff who will affect your sales. Think about your kitchen staff's receptiveness to guest tastes, your kitchen porter's appearance, your room maid's discretion, and everyone's attitude towards guest service as a whole. All will have a major impact on your guests':

- experience
- perception
- willingness to spend money
- likelihood of referring others
- prospect of returning.

So before you recruit anybody, identify the role each person has to play in helping you achieve your hotel's success. Define the values you need to reflect your identity, and the attributes you will need to recruit. Differentiate between minimum requirements and skills that can be taught.

Next, determine how you might assess or identify these values and attributes as part of your selection process. For example, if being courteous and discreet, or willing to use initiative are important attributes, you cannot judge them just by looking at an application form. You need to devise questions that test these as part of your interview process. The easiest way to do this is to ask candidates to give examples of times past when they have demonstrated these attributes.

Develop a reputation as a good employer

It's inevitable that even your most loyal team members will leave at some point. Ensure you can attract the best by developing a reputation for being a good employer.

Sadly the hospitality industry does not always get the best press, so if you are competing against other local employers for good staff you'll need people who want to apply rather than being desperate for a job.

Listen and communicate with your employees, and make them feel valued. Reward them fairly and offer good training and development, promoting from within whenever possible. This creates loyalty, reduces your staff turnover, and ultimately builds your reputation, as somewhere people want to work.

Action 9.1 Identify the attributes you need

> What are the attributes you need in each of your team members?
>
> What more can you do to build your reputation as a good place to work?

Train *all* your team in guest service

Good accommodation and food is nothing without good service. And every one of your team to some degree will impact on the guest journey.

If you've recruited the right people, it shouldn't be too difficult to achieve the standard of service you want. Everyone at some point is a customer themselves, and know how they like to be treated.

Ensure everyone understands the needs and expectations of your guest – all the aspects we discussed in Chapter 1 – so they can start to see things from the guests' perspective.

Encourage your team to take the guest journey, and see everything from a guest's point of view as often as possible; you'll be amazed at what they pick up on – things you may have grown oblivious to.

All staff should welcome guests as if it was their

own home. There shouldn't be any need for a set script, allowing staff to project some of their own personality, but do ensure that there are some basics that are always covered, dependent on the situation.

Systems and procedures

Have in place some principles or guidelines for staff to follow in specific situations, such as how guests should be greeted on arrival, what help they should be offered with their bags, offering to make dinner reservation, etc.

Establish procedures for when things go wrong: emergencies, complaints, or delays. This gives your team confidence – which your guests will notice – and provides consistency. From a financial perspective, it also safeguards you against staff giving away all your profits.

For example, in the restaurant, what is the policy if a guest complains about their meal? Depending on the nature of the complaint and the point at which the guest complains, each scenario might call for a different response. How your staff deal with it could be a key difference between a guest's negative experience, telling all their friends, and never returning; or turning the situation around so the guest comes away better off as a result (but without breaking the bank for you).

Give your team authority

The more authority and skills you give your team, the better.

From the guest's perspective, things will get dealt with more quickly, as staff don't need to find you or a manager. Telling a guest you don't have the authority to deal with an issue is both frustrating for the guest and degrading for the team member.

There will naturally be situations where a manager's input may be required, but aim to keep those to a minimum by ensuring that any one of the team can deal with the most common issues, questions or complaints.

Authority and skill give your staff a sense of responsibility, so they take more initiative in other areas. It means you don't have to keep an eye on things 24/7, in the confident knowledge that guest service will always be the best it can be.

Action 9.2 Train your team in guest service

What training do you need to give your team in guest service basics?

What systems or procedures do you need to clarify or write down so that team members can deal with them confidently?

What are the common issues that you could delegate to staff?

Take the guest journey now (and schedule it in regularly).

Involve your team in selling

To be an ambassador for your business and spot sales opportunities, every member of staff needs to know about all your services and products.

The more they know about, for example – the facilities in a room, the flexibility and capacity of the meeting room, the ingredients of a dish, how early you can get breakfast – the better placed they are to make recommendations and make a sale.

Their knowledge should not be limited to the hotel itself, but to the local amenities, attractions and directions. Staff need to know how to find out about these things if they don't know. Most importantly, make sure they are familiar with everything on your website(s), including all updates, current offers, and promotions. The guest may well have had a good read, so your staff need to know what's on the website, too.

The more of your services and products your staff can experience first-hand, the better. So ensure all your reception staff are familiar with all of your rooms and all your waiting staff have an opportunity to taste every dish on the menu. Conduct staff training in the meeting rooms so they see it as a guest would. And allow your staff to sample the treatments you provide in the spa.

Train your team how to upsell

Your front of house team needs to know how to upsell, recognise when it is appropriate to do so, and what items or services to sell.

To upsell, your staff need to:

- be able to spot the opportunities
- have confidence in their knowledge of, and be interested in the products and services on offer
- have a good understanding of the guests' needs or how to ascertain these.

Upselling is not all about trying to sell the most expensive service or product. It's about selling the most **appropriate** one. For example, if the restaurant diner is unsure of the best wine to have with their meal, it's about recommending the best match for the dish and to suit the guest's tastes, not about selling your most expensive bottle.

Or, when a guest is about to over order on side dishes, the way to build trust and rapport is to advise them that portions are big and they probably don't need to order one of each. This requires staff's confidence in their knowledge of the products and services on offer.

Staff also need to know which are the products or services that are best for the business to promote – promoting your loss leaders is not a wise strategy. So ensure front of house staff understand the products or services that make the biggest margin, and where you have a particular service or dish you want to promote to encourage follow-up sales.

Don't encourage forced sales, but do make sure any upsells are maximising profit where possible.

Keep staff updated

Recognise that a one-off training session will never be enough.

Your staff need to be kept up-to-date all the time. Conduct daily briefings with your team to cover such information as:

- VIP guests
- Special needs (e.g. disabled guests, special diets)
- Regular guests and any known preferences, so staff can anticipate their requirements
- Today's menu and tasting, with details of **all** the ingredients of **each dish**, what to promote today, and what's in short supply (even if only one dish has changed from yesterday's menu, make sure it is communicated)
- What special offers, events or deals you have coming up that need to be mentioned
- What other activity there is in the hotel or surrounding area that could affect service in any way, e.g. maintenance, road works, concerts, weather.
- Staff shortages, and cover of responsibilities

These actions ensure your staff are fully briefed and competent to deal with any guest's queries or concerns.

A daily briefing also provides an opportunity for you to get feedback on any guest comments. You can discuss any questions or suggestions your team may have about operational issues that could have a bearing on the level of service or sales potential of the hotel. So, even on your busiest mornings make sure these briefings still happen – it's generally on the days that are your busiest that things go wrong, and it's generally your busiest days when you have the best opportunities for increasing sales.

Action 9.3 Involve your team in selling

Do all your staff know **all** your products and services?

Does your front of house team know what items and services to promote **each day**?

Do **all** your team know how to upsell?

Do you conduct **daily** briefings with the team?

If not, when could you schedule these to take place?

Give responsibility

Demonstrate your trust in your team by giving them responsibility for certain tasks. This promotes ownership and will reward you with their initiative.

Feedback and improvement

A great way of encouraging continuous improvement is to encourage your team to ask for guests' feedback and what they can learn from it.

Whenever they receive feedback from guests or observe for themselves where things are not perfect, encourage them to come forward with their suggestion of **how** it can be improved, and how this will improve the guest experience. Equally, when they receive positive feedback, ask them to suggest ways to build or capitalise on this.

Develop champions

While it's important that everyone understands everyone else's job, there are some people best placed to take responsibility for certain activities, or deal with specific situations.

This promotes a sense of pride and responsibility, and will encourage continuous improvement. This in turn can have an impact on your guests' experience, when some specific knowledge is required to gain the guest's confidence – for example:

- If you are showing round a prospective wedding party, use the person with the best knowledge of the function facilities and most wedding experience.
- If your guest has a food allergy he'd probably prefer reassurances from the chef than a receptionist on the ingredients used in a dish.

Of course, everyone needs to know who is champion for what, and that you have a stand-in when this person is not available.

A team effort

Guest service and sales is a team effort, so ensure your team support one another in this.

Allocate responsibility to specific team members to conduct briefings, training, monitor results and collate feedback and suggestions. This spreads the responsibility and gets everyone involved, ensuring these happen even when you are not there. Also this allows you more time to concentrate on other things – like your sales and marketing.

Action 9.4 Give responsibility

What process can you put in place for staff to obtain and act on guests' feedback?

Who could be appointed champions for certain tasks?

How could you encourage the team to take responsibility when you are not there?

Offer staff incentives

A little incentive for staff can go a long way in making your hotel successful.

Motivate and encourage your staff to sell more,

while making guest service a priority. This will depend on good training that gives them the skills and confidence to do this in the right areas, so take the time to invest in this.

Being transparent and open about your business helps build trust and can be very eye-opening for staff.

Ensure that your staff understand your margins and how these are calculated. Without this knowledge it is all too easy for them to give away (or eat!) your profits. If they understand your budgeted margin and how well you are performing towards this, they are more likely to take some ownership and are in a stronger position to come up with ideas and contribute to your margins.

Rather than limiting incentives to a straight sales figure, you might consider a prize for the person who makes the biggest increase on their sales compared with the previous month (this incentivizes those starting from a low base). Or how about rewards for those who make the best suggestions (this includes back of house staff), and those who get the best guest feedback? Obviously, when using guest service as a metric this can be subjective, so you'll need to be clear who has judging rights here.

Ensure a fair policy for tips, service charges or tronc system that incentivises **all** team members to excellence in **all** areas that impact on the guest in some way, not just those in direct guest contact. It's very easy for waiting staff for example to 'see' the results of their efforts, but this needs to be shared and communicated to everyone in the business.

Action 9.5 Think about staff incentives

Do you give any incentive for team members to give exceptional guest service or upsell?

How effective is this in motivating all staff, in all roles or departments?

Chapter 9 recap

In this chapter we have covered:

- ✓ The importance of recruiting the **right people** and the need to develop a reputation as a good employer
- ✓ How **training** is a must for good guest service
- ✓ The need for **systems and processes** that staff can follow in specific situations
- ✓ Giving staff **authority and skill** to deal with difficult issues
- ✓ How guest service is important for **all** team members, not just front of house
- ✓ Making sure staff know **what to promote** and when to upsell
- ✓ Keeping staff constantly **up to date**, with daily briefings
- ✓ Giving staff **responsibility** for specific tasks

✓ How offering the right incentives will **encourage staff** to offer exceptional guest service and increase sales

Authors' comments

Caroline: Whenever I get involved in training staff in guest service and upselling they always come forward with lots of ideas to improve the guest experience, as well as increasing sales. If you only do one thing from this chapter take everyone (this includes you and any other managers) on the guest journey – you'll be surprised what you see once you look through a guest's eyes.

Lucy: The guest experience is very important as without it all your marketing and website efforts are wasted. Why not share your great time with guests in advance with videos on your website (staff showing what they do, testimonials from guests) and blog entries by different staff members sharing their ideas and latest news. This will demonstrate in advance how you all work as a team, and that you have some great individuals who really care about guests.

Chapter 10

Collaborating for success

Chapter 10

Collaborating for success

By now you probably have a long list of potential actions. But you don't have to go it alone.

We've already discussed getting buy-in from your team in Chapter 9, but there may be other people and businesses that can help, too.

In this chapter we'll help you identify:

- ✓ Who else you can **delegate** to in order to capitalise on their expertise
- ✓ Potential **joint venture** business partners with whom to collaborate
- ✓ How to find **affiliates** to help promote your hotel

Delegate or outsource

The chances are that you won't have the time or the expertise to do everything on your Plan, so stick with what you are good at. Find someone else who can do the parts you don't have the time or skill to do yourself.

If your time is worth £100 per hour to the hotel, and you can find someone who can do the task for £17 per hour, or even £70 per hour, and in less time, then get them to do it.

And if you don't have the expertise within your own team, look externally for someone who has. They will do it in less time, and if they have the right experience they will probably give you ideas on how to maximise your return on investment too.

Tasks you might want to outsource include: web design, email set up and mailings, copywriting, staff training, and graphic design. You'll find more about all these on our website at www.HotelSuccessHandbook.com.

Action 10.1 What to outsource

Looking at your list of actions to date, what are the areas where you don't have the expertise?

What are the actions where it might be cheaper for someone else to complete?

What are the actions that would get done more quickly or more effectively by someone else?

Partnerships and joint ventures

Other businesses already work with your ideal customers. A joint venture is when you team up or collaborate with another business or an individual to either share resources or help each other out with a promotion or service you

can't offer yourself. Joint ventures provide an ideal opportunity for some low-cost marketing.

To identify prospective joint ventures, think about other businesses that will have lists of people you would like to attract as guests. These don't have to be competitors (although many businesses do form joint ventures with their competitors quite successfully). They might be suppliers, clubs or organisations who deal with your ideal customers; other businesses who sell complementary services such as local attractions; or just fit the profile of your guests by age or location.

Joint ventures may take on many forms. The easiest joint venture is sharing your respective customer and prospect lists. You write to your entire list promoting the joint venture business, and they do the same to their list promoting you.

BUT don't just give your list to your joint venture partner. There are two reasons for this. You must be the one writing to your list, to respect the privacy of those on it. And your prospects and guests' trust is in **you**, not your partner, so when they see something coming from **you** the message has more credibility and impact. And vice versa for your partner's list. So for both privacy and effectiveness, only ever write to your own list.

Joint ventures might also be a partnership in a project. A popular option might be hosting a particular event jointly with one of your suppliers, e.g. a wine lovers' dinner, where your wine supplier provides promotional material and maybe even some of the wine in return for a speaking spot on the night. A win–win all round.

Other joint ventures may be more long-term. For example, if you are close to a particular attraction, you may be able to advertise in their promotional material and on their website (and vice versa) and for each of you to offer or give away vouchers for a discount on entry to the venue, while they give out promotional offers for your hotel. This is a way of third-party endorsement and your joint venture partner will feel a lot happier about doing this if they have had first-hand experience of what you offer, so don't be afraid to give them a taster.

Don't limit yourself to entertainment or leisure businesses, though. Think about what businesses you trade with? What businesses do your guests or prospects use? (Either locally in person or virtually online.)

This type of arrangement may even have further spin-offs, such as you providing catering, accommodation or support for big events. For example, your local tennis club runs a national tournament and recommends your hotel for accommodation (at a preferential rate), and holds its prize giving dinner at the hotel. On the other hand, if the attraction in question is something to be sought after, this may be a good selling feature for your hotel or restaurant if you're in a position to secure (maybe VIP) entry or tickets in advance.

Becoming an 'expert' opens up other opportunities for joint ventures – where do other people interested in your subject go? Think about the golf club, hobby magazine subscribers, spa product suppliers, and so on.

And don't dismiss the competition. Which other hotels or restaurants may have complementary offers, or can you refer people to when you are full and vice versa? As a hotel, recognise that your guest won't necessarily want to eat with you every night, so where do you recommend? Can a restaurant nearby offer a discount for your guests, and can you give a preferential rate for any of their diners who stay with you?

Whenever you're thinking about doing a joint venture, one thing to be clear about right up-front is the financial side of things. How much money and time will each of you be investing and how will you distribute the profits when they come in? Also, what happens if the venture is not as successful as you hoped – who will carry the financial risk? The best option here is to be transparent at the start and keep costs to the minimum required to do the job well. If you start with simply emailing each other's lists, for example, the costs are very small, but you'll quickly see any results.

Find affiliates

Affiliates are similar to joint ventures but can be a lot easier to set up, especially where arrangements are already in place – typically online.

An affiliate is someone who will earn a commission

from you for any referral business that results in a sale, or you can sell their products or services in return for commission.

Potential affiliates might be any of the examples given for joint ventures or, in addition: bookshops selling maps and local literature, art galleries, and equipment hire (e.g. bicycles, fishing gear, hiking boots, minicab or private tour hire).

There are a host of affiliate 'brokers' online who allow you to sign up your website and add any of their affiliate network to your site according to agreed guidelines and commission structures.

If you want to **offer car hire, travel insurance, luggage for sale, books or films**, for example, there is already likely to be an affiliate programme set up that you can join and earn commissions from right away.

This isn't just about you making some more 'money' from your website however, and you shouldn't look at it this way. Instead, see it as a way to **add value** to your guests and help them. If they can book and buy not just their holiday from your website but other products and services related to it, they save time and you've offered them a better service.

Ideas for joint ventures and affiliates

Here are just a few ideas you could use as joint ventures or affiliates, all of which add value for your guests and benefits the third party.

Local businesses

- If your perfect customers include locals in your bar, restaurant or for functions, which **local businesses** already sell to this target market?
- **Hairdressers, spas, beauty salons** – sell their gift vouchers, or offer guests complimentary rates or inclusive deals
- Sell **other business gift vouchers** online as an affiliate at a discounted rate if bought in advance
- **Taxi firms** – provide transport to and from station or airport
- **Florists** to give flower arranging demonstrations and you earn a commission on any sales
- **Galleries** to display artworks for sale in the hotel
- **Prize draw or competitions** to win their products or services (These could be local or national if there's a chain in their home town)
- If you do **weddings**, what arrangements can you make with photographers, printers (for wedding stationery) florists, jewellers, and

wedding car hire firms?

- If your target market is **business people** what joint ventures could you arrange with local businesses to supply business lunches and/or meeting facilities at special rates in return for all their accommodation requirements?

Suppliers

- **Wine suppliers** to set up wine tastings and supply wines for a wine lovers' dinner or weekend
- Your **butcher or greengrocer** to supply hampers or take-away boxes for people to take home
- Local businesses to give **demonstrations of their crafts** e.g. cheese makers, florists, cake decorators

Affiliate links

- **Hire shops** e.g. fishing gear, bicycles – set up affiliate links on your site for your guests to pre-book at a preferential rate and you earn a commission
- **Bookshops**, for guests to purchase maps and books of local interest that you have recommended, also films that either feature your local area, or are your recommendations.
- Your **linen** or **toiletries** suppliers for guests to buy personalised products

Attractions

- Include entry to one or more attractions as part of a package
- Ask the attractions to promote your hotel as the best place to stay, and offer 'specials' to their visitors, e.g. free shuttle bus to the attraction
- Ask attraction to email to their list with your offer and promotions

Expert topic

Talk to **clubs, societies, suppliers** and **magazines** that cover your topic to:

- Have them send your offers and promotions to their lists or members
- Invite them as guests to themed weekends, mini breaks or workshops
- Set up affiliate links for any products they sell online
- Arrange visits to their venues for private tours, demonstrations or exclusive shopping evenings.

Sports, clubs and societies

- To give a demonstration or talk on the topic
- Provide special rate season tickets or temporary memberships (weekly for holiday guests or annual for business guests) to use their facilities

- Special rates on hire of equipment

Theme weekends, mini breaks or holidays based around specialist club activities

This could apply to any of the above categories.

- You both promote the events to your lists
- Guest speakers from the club at special dinners
- Exclusive use of their facilities for the duration
- Special trips arranged to other venues of interest on the same theme
- Quizzes, games night, competitions based on the topic
- Exclusive shopping trips either on or off site

Competitors

- Share lists with other hotels who have the same guest profile, but in different parts of the country or world
- Set up an 'overflow' arrangement with fellow hotels in the area to recommend when you are fully booked, and vice versa
- Share the cost of setting up promotions, equipment hire and specialist input if you'd generate enough business for both to benefit.

Action 10.2 Mindmap your joint ventures and affiliates

Using the mind map below, brainstorm what options you have for joint ventures and affiliates. Aim to have at least three ideas for each heading, but don't stop at three if you have more ideas!

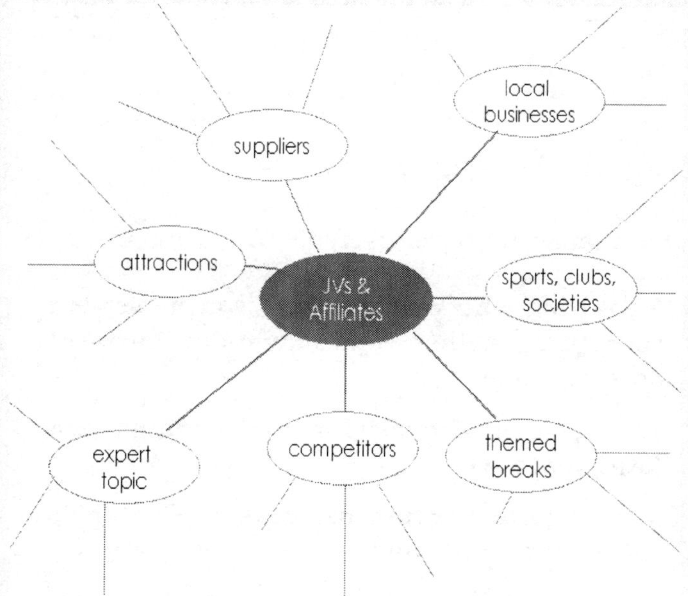

Now for each potential joint venture or affiliate, identify at least two projects or ideas you could do with them which will appeal to your ideal guest, and be of benefit to both you and the joint venture partner.

Action 10.3 Bring it all together

Now update your plan with all your ideas from this chapter.

Who have you identified as potential joint venture partners or affiliates?

What further research do you need to verify these ideas?

Chapter 10 recap

In this chapter we have covered:

- ✓ Identifying **who else** can help you implement your plan so that your day-to-day business does not suffer
- ✓ The value of establishing **partnerships and joint ventures**
- ✓ Identify **joint venture partners** who can help your business and achieve a **win-win**

Authors' comments

Caroline: Lots of the managers I work with find it hard to let go, and as a result end up trying to do everything at considerable cost to themselves and the success of the hotel. I probably devote more of my time with coaching clients on this topic than anything else. Start by identifying what you want to achieve, then delegate and learn to trust others.

Lucy: A phrase that I've always revered as great business advice is 'stick to your knitting' – meaning don't try and be jack of all trades and master of none when it comes to your business. It's very important that you know where you want to go, and what you want to do with your hotel but that does **not** mean you should do it all! Use experts, delegate and work with partners so that you can concentrate on what you're good at.

There are some more resources on this topic on our website www.HotelSuccessHandbook.com

Chapter 11

Bringing it all together

Chapter 11

Bringing it all together

Now it's time to bring everything we've looked at together in a plan. Not – we hasten to add – something written in tablets of stone, but a working document where you can monitor progress, track results and adjust accordingly.

Marketing is never a one-off activity, so use a format for your plan that you can add to. Build in milestones, measurements and review points and be prepared to change and add to your plan as necessary – it will evolve.

Set goals

It's highly unlikely you will want to do every single idea and action we've covered (or at least not all at once!), so having set goals makes it easy to see what actions are right for your business right now, what to try later, and what aren't a fit.

So the first step is to have some clearly defined goals in mind, and once you have these you can formulate a strategy to achieve them.

You probably have a good idea of what you want to achieve and how you 'see' your business working, but is this written down? Do you have specific goals, actions and a plan that you refer to all the time? Bearing in mind that the market does not stand still Your business plan can't stand still either. What made sense just six months ago, might not now.

Now's the time to refer back to your criteria for success from the first exercise (Action 0.1) and set some milestones based on the initial goals you set. If you are looking at a 5-year goal this can be a bit daunting, so break this down into what to achieve over the next 12 months, the next 6 months and then the next 4 weeks. This way you end up with manageable chunks, but still leading up to the master plan all focused towards your ultimate criteria for success.

Be clear about what you want to achieve. If you want to increase occupancy rates – what level are they now, and what rate do you want to achieve; if you want to increase profit – how much profit do you want to make? Is this net or gross, before or after tax, and in what time frame? The more specific you are the better.

What's possible

Before we get stuck into goals you need to get excited about what is possible and what can be achieved in your business. Here's some simple maths (and please be assured it is simple and we've used illustrations – so don't stop reading just yet!) to demonstrate how just little changes can make a difference to your profits.

Now looking at numbers may not sound exciting to everyone (we're with you there!) BUT numbers are vital for understanding your hotel, and also how to measure its success, and the success of any actions you implement.

You may remember in the introduction we talked about the three things you need to increase:

- the number of guests
- the average sale per guest
- the numbers of sales per guest

What most businesses do is only focus on one area.

Let's work through a simple example to see what happens when you do this. Imagine you have 500 guests, the average 'sale' is £100, and they come to you on average twice a year.

No of guests	Average spend	No of visits	Total income
500	100	2	100,000

So if we take a very general (and common) business objective of **increasing sales**, by increasing the number of guests here is how just small changes can affect that:

If you increase the number of guests by 10% you

will get a 10% increase in income.

No of guests	Average spend	No of visits	Total income
550	100	2	110,000

Equally, if you increase either the average spend **or** the average number of visits by 10% you'll still get a 10% increase in income.

But look what happens if you increase **all three** by 10%...

No of guests	Average spend	No of visits	Total income
550	110	2.2	133,100

This equates to a **massive 33.1% increase** across the board, as opposed to just 10% if you were to only focus on the number of guests.

So your three key questions are:

- How do I increase the **number of guests?**
- How do I increase the **sale per guest?** i.e. the room rate and additional purchases?
- How do I increase the **number of sales** per guest, i.e. the duration of their stay and the number of times each guest returns?

It is probably easier to think in terms of one sale being one unit of booking – so if you sell rooms by the night then one night equals one unit; if you sell rooms by the week then one week equals one unit.

But back to the numbers...

What does this mean? Well, working with only one of the actions gives you linear growth, while looking at all 3 simultaneously can give you exponential growth (i.e. a lot more!).

And if this hasn't got you excited yet – let's look at the **profit implication** of these changes...

With a 10% increase across the board we'll assume that most fixed costs are likely to stay about the same. So if we just take it that variable costs go up proportionately let's look at another example:

	Existing income	With 33.1% increase
Turnover	100,000	133,100
Fixed costs	40,000	40,000
Variable costs	40,000	53,240
Gross profit	20,000	39,240

This is **nearly 100% increase in profit**, based on 50% of costs being variable. At this point you may be saying that a 10% increase in any of these areas is ambitious, but even if you just made just a 2% increase based on the figures above, that would still give you an **18% increase** in profit.

Action

Run through your business accounts and have a play with what differences a change in profits to any of these numbers could make.

If you want some help there's an Excel spreadsheet you can download from our website (www.HotelSuccessHandbook.com), which you can put your numbers into to see the results.

You may already do year to date comparisons, and budget planning, but it's always a good idea to run through some scenarios that small changes can make. Even if you already think you have all the numbers you need – it can help by just looking at some in isolation and not in the usual format you normally see them in. Don't skip this step – it's important to have a clear, real and achievable result in your mind when you plan your strategy and actions.

Now you can see what's possible with the numbers – you'll be able to focus on how to get those numbers to be real.

Your business goals

What are your targets? Decide which metrics or Key Performance Indicators (KPIs) you want to use for your hotel, e.g.

- Number of guests
- Average spend per stay
- Average duration
- Average frequency/number of visits per annum
- Occupancy levels
- Average daily room rate
- Revenue per available room
- Total sales turnover
- Gross profit
- Net profit before tax

Remember, stick to one or two measures that you can monitor easily on a monthly or weekly basis.

Now, whichever metrics you decide to use, you need to know your starting point, so you can gauge your progress. If you don't already know this information – it's time to find out.

What do you want to achieve for your business?

Write down the business goals for your hotel in exact terms and numbers to see in black and white what you are aiming for. Make the goals realistic, but don't make them too easy.

- Increase sales turnover from £ ___ to £ ___
- Increase occupancy levels from ___ % to ___ %
    - New guests
    - Repeat business
    - At specific times of the year
- Increase revenue per available room (RevPAR) from £ ___ to £ ___
- Increase the average spend per head per stay from £ ___ to £ ___
- Increase gross profit from £ ___ to £ ___
- Gain an ____ % return on all marketing activity

Action 11.1 Identify business goals

What I want the to achieve for the business:

Your Hotel Success Plan

Now it's time to review all the answers to the exercises you've recorded as you went through this book. What ideas have you generated by each exercise? How will each of these contribute towards your goals? Is there anything else you've missed to add to the list for a later date?

We realise it's very unlikely you can do everything at once; time and resources won't allow this, and there are things you'll want to get right first. There will also be some activities that will get a better result at different times e.g. seasonal events. Just remember marketing is an ongoing activity, so you want to be able to implement ideas over a period of time, not all at once.

Think about your quick wins, i.e. the things that you could implement really quickly and easily to get the ball rolling. This will not only give you a quick return, but also inspire you and motivate you to continue with your marketing efforts. Even small changes can make a big difference and will also give you confidence to try more.

There is often no way to know for sure if **your** guests will respond to an offer or marketing approach until you try and test it, so you need to be bold. And if something is not working review why, and either change it or stop doing it. You can't make this choice unless you are **tracking your results** – we can't stress this enough. Make sure your website analytics are in place, you have a way of recording enquiries and guest information, and that you know your numbers.

Action 11.2 Update your plan

Now update your initial plan, and add in priorities and dates. There is a template in the resources area of www.HotelSuccessHandbook.com

Identify your first action and get started

You can't do it all at once, so now chose from the action plan which items could give you some quick wins? i.e. for a small amount of effort now could pay some dividends in a short space of time? Define what you want to achieve, and then think about all the steps you will need to take to achieve this.

Action 11.3 Add in the detail

Highlight just one thing to get you started – don't be too ambitious at this point – better to get the ball rolling on just one thing and do it well.

Do you have a goal for this action?

Have you identified how you will evaluate it?

If so, now break this down into all the actions needed to achieve this.

Now schedule these into your diary including any review dates.

PUT YOUR PLAN INTO ACTION!

Chapter 11 recap

- ✓ Start with **written** goals for your hotel
- ✓ Work at increasing guests, frequency of visits **and** spend per head in tandem
- ✓ Implement only those ideas that will help to achieve **your goals**
- ✓ Be **selective** and don't try and implement everything at once
- ✓ Start with some quick wins for instant returns and confidence building
- ✓ Measure your success against your KPIs, refer to your analytics, and numbers to 'see' your results

So now it's time to put your Hotel Success Plan into action.

Here's to your Hotel Success

Enjoy!

Caroline and Lucy

Glossary

advertorial Form of print advert designed to look like an article in the magazine or newspaper.

alt tags Alternative text that relates to an image on a website which describes the image and will be displayed if the image does not show. Screen reader programmes use them for the visually impaired. They are important for coping with different website browser settings in case the image cannot be displayed.

analytics Statistics that give you website information, e.g. keywords used, site referred from, pages visited, how long visitors have stayed on your site.

below the fold The bottom of a website page that can't be seen on screen unless the reader scrolls down. Content here sometimes gets missed.

blog Short for web-log, a specific type of website regularly updated with news, events, opinions, its origins being in a diary style. Blogs are hosted on their own website platforms (e.g. WordPress) and are very quickly picked up by search engines.

browser Software used to access website in the Internet e.g. Internet Explorer, Firefox, Safari.

call to action The prompt in any marketing messages that tell your what to do next e.g. phone us on this number, fill in the form, book now...

clickthrough The action of clicking through from an online advert to your website.

CMS Content management system – online software for building and managing a website that allows you to update your own website easily without going back to the designer.

conversion rate The number of enquires that convert to bookings or sales, expressed as a percentage.

crawling Describes how the search engines scan your website for listing.

Facebook Social media website.

Gross margin Income from sales, less cost of sales.

frequency Number of times customers or guests return and buy again.

joint venture When you team up with another business or an individual to either share resources or help each other out with a promotion or service you can't offer yourself.

landing pages A destination page on your website specific to an offer or campaign. Can be a stand-alone page, or part of your main website.

LinkedIn Social media website for business contacts.

loss leader A service or product you sell at very low profit margin or loss which draws customers, in the hope that they will spend money on other high profit items.

media-rich content Having photos, video, audio as part of your website (opposed to just text) to add to the visitor experience of your site and appeal to people's preferences for information.

microsite Small websites with just a few pages.

natural search Results that appear in the search engine results that are not paid for.

net margin Income from sales, less all operating costs (fixed and variable).

opt-in When a customer ticks a box to say they would like to be on your mailing list. Double or confirmed opt-in is when you send them a link and they click on the link to confirm.

PDF Portable document format – a way to print documents, brochures and leaflets to send online.

PPC Pay per click – advertising links in search engines where the advertiser pays every time someone clicks through to their site.

PR Public relations.

qualified traffic Website traffic that fits your customer profile/target market.

quick win Small actions you can implement with little time and effort to achieve a big change.

retweet (RT) Forwarding someone else's message on Twitter.

search engine How you find out more about the topic that interests you – e.g. Google, Yahoo!

SEO Search engine optimisation – using keywords that people will use to find you in search engines like Google.

Sponsored links Results that appear in search engine listings as a result of PCC campaigns

title tags The title you give to an image to help with search engine optimisation.

traffic The number of people who visit your website.

tweet Message on Twitter of up to 140 characters.

Twitter Social media website.

USP Unique selling point or proposition.

vanity phrases A generic key word or phrase you may want to appear under for search engine results or PPC results, but is too general and therefore has too much competition or results in unqualified traffic.

WordPress Blog software platform on which it is possible to build anything from a blog to a full website using as a CMS (content management system).

YouTube Video hosting website.

To access all the resources mentioned in the book go to www.HotelSuccessHandbook.com

We've got templates, lists and information ready for you to download on the website that will help you build your hotel success plan.

We'll also be adding updates, new ideas and extra hints & tips via our website so if you sign up you'll be the first to hear about them.

Chapter 3. Mission statement on home page.
Explain why FCA different from competitors, promote areas. More detailed info on additional page via hyperlinks. FCA History (about us page), Info tags on photos
You tube channel? Create PDF's that guests can print
outsider feedback on website (questions for them to find out)
alternate ways of booking from base nav button
Chat service - assign specific times RV day), Landing pages for specific events, Microsites (one for each ind property)

Chapter 4/5 Headlines for good copy (use for package pages)
Images of packages + everything provided. 10 rooms @ or first 10 to book deals with updates of how many left
Deadline window bookings noting how fast it sells out
Vouchers to buy (£125 for £100) + use as part payment on booking form. Months prize draw for bookings 30 days ahead get additional items. Links to press releases or testimonials
Gift Vouchers. networking event for non booking companies
upgrades for longer stays. Guarantee ideas. How did you hear about us on booking form. Online article sites + forums.
Blogs good for SEO. Tickets for Castle Concerts.

Chapter 8 - RV rewards (must stay x amount in x years) RW rewards for referrals. Personal rewards + offers for RV corps. Birthday vouchers. Promos in lift + flyers. Booker rewards. Offer of the month

Lightning Source UK Ltd.
Milton Keynes UK
UKOW031006210212

187672UK00001B/20/P

9 781904 312888

other hyperlink to what "serviced" means / leisure package gym cinema dinner / free Sunday / Rugby package / Highland Show package / Birthday Breaks / facebook only promo